Omer Tanghe

AS I HAVE LOVED YOU

Catherine de Hueck Doherty
and
Her Spiritual Family

VERITAS

English language edition
First published 1988 by
Veritas Publications
7-8 Lower Abbey Street
Dublin 1

Original Dutch language edition first published by
Drukkerij-Uitgeverij Lannoo pvba,
Tielt
Belgium

ISBN 1 85390 055 9

Cover design: Eddie McManus
Typesetting by: Printset & Design Ltd., Dublin
Printed in the Republic of Ireland by
Mount Salus Press Ltd., Dublin

CONTENTS

As I Have Loved You, Catherine de Hueck Doherty and Her Spiritual Family, was originally published in Belgium by Lannoo/tielt/weesp, 1985, under the title ZOALS IK U HEB LIEFGEHAD, *Catherine Doherty en haar Poustinia-volgelingen.* It has been translated by Omer Tanghe and Robert Wild. Special thanks to Mary Ruth for her editorial assistance.

TRANSLATOR'S NOTE

In this book[1] Father Omer Tanghe describes the life of
Catherine de Hueck Doherty and her followers. Catherine died
on 14 December 1985, at the age of eighty-nine. She was one
of the first lay people in our century to put into practice the social
doctrine of the Church, and to answer the call of the popes to
live the gospel without compromise among the poor and the
lonely. In the 1930s she became the advocate for equal rights
for the poor, and especially for the black people of America. Her
bold preaching of the gospel disturbed many people. She lived
among the poor in the slums of major cities, and gradually
developed a new spirituality for the lay apostolate.

In 1947 she went to Combermere in Ontario, Canada, and
there founded Madonna House, a Training Centre for the Lay
Apostolate. Every year hundreds of young people and adults
come to Combermere to discover a meaning for their lives. The
influence of Madonna House in the universal Church is growing
steadily. It already has a place of specific importance among
contemporary spirituality groups.

1. The Dutch language edition was published a few months
   before Catherine's death.

ABOUT THE AUTHOR

Father Omer Tanghe is a priest of the diocese of Bruges in Belgium. He has a master's degree in missiology and has done post-graduate studies on the developing countries at the Catholic University of Louvain. He is the director of the Pontifical Mission Aid Societies in his diocese, and is an associate priest of Madonna House.

Father Tanghe is well-known in his country, being the author of twenty-six books on mission and contemporary spiritualities. Among other topics, he has written books on Mother Teresa of Calcutta, on the arctic missionaries of Canada, on new movements in the Church in India and the Middle East. One of his most popular books concerned 'ordinary priests, sisters, and laity' whose daily, simple dedication forms the backbone of the Church's life. One book, *Prayers From Life*, has been published in English by P.J. Kenedy and Sons, New York, 1968.

As mission director for his diocese, Father Tanghe has visited many countries, giving lectures and conferences on missiology. In his contacts with the 'Third Church' he sees many hopeful signs for the future of the Church. He considers Madonna House his spiritual family. In his talks he often shares with others Catherine's profound teachings on the Christian life today.

INTRODUCTION

INTRODUCING FATHER TANGHE AND MADONNA HOUSE

by
Archbishop Joseph Raya
and
Father Emile Briere

It was in Nazareth, fifteen years ago, that I introduced Father Omer Tanghe to the Mother Church of all the churches. I bestowed upon him the honour of Archimandrite, which made him a member of the Church of Galilee.

Nazareth is the town of the Incarnation where God assumed our human flesh and became one with us, became our High Priest, the Priest of all creation. In Nazareth, Father Omer deepened his awareness of the priesthood of Christ.

In Nazareth Father Omer became acquainted with the spirituality of the Fathers and acquired a great love for the theology and spirituality of the Eastern Church. Born in Flanders, nourished by the generosity and tenderness of heart of his noble Flemish ancestry, he found in the Eastern Church a new source of inspiration.

From Nazareth he spread his wings to the Far East and met Mother Theresa and her works of goodness to humanity.

From Nazareth he also flew to the Far West, to the wilderness of Canada, and met another giant of the Church in the person of Catherine de Hueck Doherty, the foundress of the Madonna House Apostolate. Catherine Doherty was the perfect example of a theologian and spiritual writer, integrating Western theology and spirituality into her Eastern Church soul. In her, East joined West in perfect harmony.

The 'B', as we affectionately called her, was, indeed, the image of the noble human being; of the Christian who found her way to the Kingdom of God on earth. She gave up all her possessions and the comforts of riches to dedicate her life to the poor and the destitute of this world. Long before the official Church had implemented its teaching on social justice, Catherine was in the slums of Toronto, Harlem and Chicago's west side, preaching love and peace among the downtrodden black people and the poor.

All the missions of Madonna House are characterised by the glorious generosity of the Gospel expressed through poverty, chastity and obedience. The spirits and lives of these lay people and priests are completely at the service of humanity, witnessing to the dignity and divine worth of the human person.

As I Have Loved You is a mirror reflecting the miracles of love and the beauty of the face of Christ, shining in the faces of those who have consecrated their lives to this apostolate. Father Omer Tanghe is one of these.

I bless this work, and all those who will read and meditate upon the glorious face of Christ in the faces of his followers. May they delight and rejoice in this book.

Archbishop Joseph Raya
Combermere, 1986

*   *   *   *   *

Several years before her death Catherine was compelled, by her failing health, to transfer her responsibilities for Madonna House to her spiritual children. Her health had become very poor, but she filled her days and nights with prayers as never before. Whoever joined her in St Catherine's Hermitage, where she lived, experienced the power of this prayer. The love she poured forth from her sick bed was reciprocated by her friends and by the members of Madonna House.

Her message has not changed. Before she died she asked Father Omer to share the following with all who would read this book: 'Do not fail to love God unconditionally, since he loves you so dearly. Love each other and serve each other. Have an unbounded faith in the Theotokos, the Mother of God. To the end of her life she proclaimed the message of St John's gospel: 'This is my command, that you love one another as I have loved you.' She also asked of all who would read this book: 'Pray for me, please pray for me.'

Emile Briere,
Priest of Madonna House
St Catherine's Hermitage
Madonna House, Combermere
Easter, 7 April 1985

1

COMBERMERE
AND MADONNA HOUSE

The long line of passengers waiting for the Toronto-Pembroke bus at the downtown Toronto bus station usually consists of some business people, country people, young people, and a few foreigners with a label on their suitcases reading 'Combermere'.

Combermere, a small village in the Madawaska Valley, lies on the road between Toronto and Pembroke, 300 kilometres north-east of Toronto. It takes five hours to get there from Toronto. You travel by bus along Lake Ontario and just before you reach Newcastle you veer north in the direction of Peterborough. You continue north beyond Peterborough through Lakefield, Burleigh Falls, Bancroft, and then Combermere. The region north of Peterborough is sparsely settled, strewn with scores of small lakes and rivers. There are a few scarcely visible farms which are almost hidden behind the ridges of wooded and hilly countryside.

Combermere was named after the English Lord Combermere, whose youngest son emigrated in 1790 to the plot of land with which the family was presented by the British Crown. It is now a village of a few hundred inhabitants, among whom are numerous Polish immigrants who earn their livelihoods in the lumber industry, or by farming the rather poor and rocky land, or in some tourist-related business such as summer cabins.

The ruggedness of the countryside is beautiful and spellbinding. The mountains which enclose the valley are part of the Laurentians, the oldest mountain range in the world. Twenty or thirty miles to the north you can visit Algonquin Provincial Park. The names of many of the rivers, creeks, hills, and valleys derive from the Indian tribes who populated this area in the past. South-east, the 150-mile Madawaska River, on which Combermere is situated, joins the Ottawa River. It was along this river that the Jesuit Fathers had their missions in the seventeenth century, and it is also believed that they were in the Madawaska Valley as well. In 1648 and 1667 the French missionaries (including John de Breboeuf and Isaac Jogues) were killed by the Indians.

The climate in and around Combermere, situated on a plateau 1000 feet above sea level, is severe. From November to the end of April the winters are very harsh with temperatures as low as -35° Fahrenheit. They are followed by three months of mild spring weather and a summer which can be hot and oppressive. The blackflies and mosquitos can be a nightmare! Autumn is a beautiful season with wonderful shades of colour in the leaves and shrubs, harbingers of winter. This is the 'Indian summer', the period when the Indians left the woods and hunting fields and went south to their winter quarters.

The bus stops in front of the post office which was rebuilt and enlarged not too long ago to cope with the increased flow of letters and correspondence to and from Madonna House. Visitors are met at the bus stop each night by a member of the community, and are taken to Madonna House which is situated a mile further down Route 517 in a wooded area on an inlet of the Madawaska.

A small sign out front says, 'Madonna House, Training Centre for the Lay Apostolate'. On a telephone pole in front of the main house there is another sign which reads, 'Welcome Pilgrim'. If you turned slightly to your left you would see the apple orchard and a small flower garden. On one of the trees is still another plaque which reads:

> This orchard was planted by
> Eddie and Catherine Doherty
> and their good neighbors
> Diseary Mayhew and Wilfred
> Bouchard.
> May 17, 1947

It is at this very spot that Catherine de Hueck Doherty and her husband Eddie arrived on 17 May 1947. They moved into the small house where, ever since, an important part of Church history has continued to be lived and written.

Madonna House: Training Centre for the Lay Apostolate
As you leave the parking lot and head for the main house you will see a huge pole with the names of all the places in the world where Madonna House has missions. The majority are in North America, but there are also houses in Barbados, England and

France. The main entrance to Madonna House is through a basement door. This lower level contains the cloakroom, TV/recreation area, and part of the library. If you didn't enter here but walked around to the front of the house, facing the river, you would get a better idea of the original, six-room, small wooden house. The front door is painted blue, in honour of Our Lady, and over it is a large blue cross with the words 'PAX CARITAS'. This view is a better reminder of the early years of Catherine's Combermere adventure.

The dining room of the original house (now called the 'little library') looks out over the Madawaska River. It contains icons, souvenirs Catherine brought from Russia, and many books on eastern spirituality and Russian history and literature. In the course of the years a large kitchen was added to this house. Here, the regular meals are prepared for 100 or so people three times a day every day. Also added in later years was a large dining room/library and, upstairs, a chapel.

Near the parking lot is a garage where goods donated to Madonna House are stored until they can be sorted. In the same general area is a large building called St Goupil's, after the Jesuit martyr. It houses a women's dormitory, an office, a sewing and laundry room and, downstairs, a maintenance work-place.

On the way to the new chapel of Our Lady of the Woods is a religious museum. Catherine has a good sense of history. She has collected many religious articles of Catholic devotional life — pictures, statues, vestments, etc. She has always taught that people should not forget their roots. The museum is like a catechetical visual aid. It reminds older Catholics of their religious past, and the young are instructed in their heritage.

Upon leaving the parking lot, if you did not go into the main house but crossed the road, you would see a variety of buildings: St Martha's, with office downstairs and dormitory upstairs; Our Lady Seat of Wisdom, the new second-hand book shop; St Germaine's, the dormitory for visiting female guests; St Raphael's, the handicraft centre; the gift shop where both donated and community-made goods are sold for the benefit of the poor; finally, there is a museum of the local culture.

If you headed back across the road, but turned right, down the road, instead of going across, you would come first to St Julia's, which houses the women applicants (those preparing to become community members). Next to that is St Luke's, the dispensary.

A few hundred yards further down is the local parish church of the Canadian Martyrs, and next to it the cemetery where Catherine, her husband Fr Eddie, Fr Callahan, and several other members of Madonna House are buried.

Two miles down the same road is another piece of property called Carmel Hill. A few hundred yards from the main highway you will see six new poustinias, situated along a hilly ridge, overlooking the valley like sentinels. Finally, you will come to Carmel Hill proper which includes the priests' guest house, some storage barns, the archives building, Archbishop Raya's house, a men's dormitory and, further back, the men applicants' dormitory (St Robert's), and several poustinias for the use of the priests.

Returning to the main highway, and proceeding three miles further, you come to St Benedict's Acres, the community's farm. There is a central house which once belonged to two trappers, and later to three teachers and their families. It is surrounded by sheds, barns, a maintenance garage, a food-processing house, and a dairy house where cheese is made. The farm produces most of the food needed to supply the community and any visitors with vegetables, grains, cheese, eggs, milk, butter, and a limited amount of meat (served mostly on Sundays). Upstairs in the main house is a chapel, where Mass is celebrated daily for the men who live at the farm.

On the way back to Madonna House in Combermere you would pass still another piece of property called Marian Meadows. Besides several poustinias for the use of the men, the community's pre-seminarian programme is situated there. Several years ago, through Catherine's inspiration, the community offered itself as a place where young men could come to experience the simple way of life before entering the seminary. One of the priests and a staff member live in this house together with several young men sent here by their Canadian Bishops.

Back down at the main house there is an area of land called 'the island'. Until their new chapel was built this island (peninsula, really) was accessible only by a bridge; now there is a road leading into it. Here is their new (1972) chapel of Our Lady of the Woods, built with logs in the local style, and topped with a Russian-Byzantine dome. Here the community gathers daily for morning prayer and for Eucharist in the evening.

Surrounding this chapel, and hidden by the trees, are poustinias where some of the priests live as poustinikki; poustinias

18

for daily use by the women; another cabin where a woman paints icons; and still another where one of the women lives as a poustinik.

In a corner of this island, in view of both the river and the main house, is Catherine's cabin, known as St Catherine's (or, affectionately, as St Kate's). Nearby is her own smaller poustinia, St George's, and a small, Russian-style shrine to Our Lady of Kazan.

Finally, to complete the picture, a mile or so towards the town of Combermere is St Joseph's mission house of several women who serve the local people more directly with a clothing room and simple hospitality. A few miles from there is Cana Colony where, during the summer months, families come together with one of the Madonna House priests to experience a week of the community's spirituality.

The town of Combermere itself is very small. It is situated in a rugged area of woods, hills, and very rocky terrain. But it is here that these men and women of Madonna House amaze the world with their way of life as a family centred on God. They are like a group of contemporary monks who, for God's sake, have accepted poverty and prayer as true values in their lives.

On my last visit before Catherine died one of the community pointed to her cabin and said, 'This cabin, where our foundress is living and awaiting her death, is a holy place'. During the last year or so of her life, if you had been fortunate enough to visit Catherine in this cabin, she would often talk to you about prayer, or about God who loves us so much and with whom she was in love. 'I am in love with God', she used to say.

This is the deep secret of Madonna House; the members of the community are in love with God. But to have a greater understanding of the community, you must know more about the interesting career and personality of its foundress, Catherine de Hueck Doherty.

2

CATHERINE de HUECK DOHERTY: FRAGMENTS FROM HER LIFE

From Russia to Canada

Catherine Kolychkine was born on the feast of the Assumption, 15 August 1896, in a Pullman car, at Nijni-Novgorod (now Gorki) in Russia, where her family had gone to visit the Great Fair. Her father held an important position at the Tsar's court, and fulfilled diplomatic missions in Egypt, Turkey, Greece and France. Catherine therefore received a universal education, and at the age of fifteen could already speak several languages.

The family's home town was St Petersburg which, at the beginning of this century, was one of the most intellectual and cultural cities of Europe. The names of Dostoevsky, Tchaikovsky, Borodin, Rimsky-Korsakov, Tolstoy, Gogol, Pushkin and many others, are connected with this city.

In her youth, Catherine was influenced by the whole of Russian culture, and by the particular way in which the Russians put the Gospel into practice. The deep Gospel piety of her family, the pomp and splendour of the Russian Orthodox liturgy, the very 'earthy' devotion of the Russian people — sinners, sceptics and saints — all gave Catherine an intimacy with the traditions and symbols of the Christian East:

> Every Easter, whenever possible, my father, mother and I, and later my brother Serge, used to go to Jerusalem for the Holy Week ceremonies. My mother was Orthodox, and she followed very carefully all the liturgies of the Orthodox Church. She especially liked the liturgy of the burial of Christ.
>
> Father liked to bring home some of the olive oil from the Garden of Gethsemane. He had strong feelings about how everyone had abandoned Christ there; he often spoke about it. So in our house there was always a big quart bottle of this blessed oil from the Garden of Gethsemane. I inherited a great devotion to the passion of Christ from my father and mother.

One day my parents took me to the rock of the Ascension, the place near Jerusalem from which Christ arose into heaven. I loved to look at that rock because it showed the imprints of the feet of Christ. But was a bit difficult, because they had this area cordoned off. But what's a rope to a little girl? One day I just slid underneath while everybody was praying, and put my little feet into these imprints, one up and the other down.

People began screaming, 'Look what she's doing! Look what she's doing! Get the child out of here! Blasphemy, blasphemy!' A Russian priest came out and said, 'Let the little children come to me, have you forgotten that?' He helped me put my feet in the imprints of the feet of Jesus Christ and then he escorted me out of there.

This aristocractic child, from her earliest years, was initiated by her mother in the things of everyday life. She learned cooking, sewing, laundering, gardening, how to run a house, how to take on responsibility and administration. Besides this, she rode horses, skied, and was taught to be a sensitive and artistic woman. Catherine's thoughts and actions in later life were clearly marked by all these influences. They began with her family life in Russia and deepened through the foreign cultures in which she lived.

At the age of fifteen she was married to a wealthy man, Boris de Hueck. Two years later, in 1917, when Russia and Germany were at war, she went to the front as a nurse. There she was decorated for her courage and self-sacrifice. However, after the October revolution, she and her husband, as members of aristocratic families, had to flee abroad, and suffered the terrors of pursuit, civil war, and near starvation.

In their flight from Russia they came to Kiskila, a village just over the Finnish border. They immediately found themselves in the hands of the communists who condemned them to die of starvation. They were saved in the nick of time by the Finnish authorities, but memories of this experience of starvation were to remain with Catherine all her life:

Yes, I remember all these things and sometimes I still dream about them. But thank God for that experience because I can identify with the hungry. This is why it is difficult for me to see people stuffing themselves with food. I always hear in the background, 'Remember? Remember when you starved? They eat too much. They eat too much.'

From Finland they went to England, and in 1920 they finally arrived in Canada. They were destitute and would have to care for a baby that was on the way. Boris' health had been badly undermined by all the privations he had endured. While he looked for some light engineering work in Montreal, Catherine, on the advice of the parish priest, Father McCabe, went to look for a job in New York which would provide her with some means of helping to maintain the family. Father McCabe was the pastor of St Clare's Church in north Toronto where Catherine's son, George, had been baptised, and where she was then living.

In New York she became washerwoman, servant, waitress and shop assistant. In this way she came into direct contact with the poor and the drop-outs of a large city. This is how she described the circumstances to which she was now brought:

> I asked the girls I worked with there where they roomed. They said Charles Street, the street which leads to the Hudson River and the waterfront. It was down town. I asked, 'Do you think I can get a room there?' 'Oh, yes,' they said, 'you can get a piece of a bed because one girl left.'
>
> That's how I met Ma Murphy, a good Catholic woman whose husband was a tugboat captain. Her boardinghouse was a three-story affair, with the girls on the top floor and her tugboat husband in the middle. Stevedores rented rooms on the first floor.
>
> So I rented a 'piece of bed', literally. There were three girls to a bed, six to a room, each paying a dollar a week to Mrs Murphy. I sent two dollars a week for George in Toronto, and kept four. Not very much, really, to live on.
>
> All of us walked every day from Charles Street to 14th, about a mile or so. It wore out the shoes, but shoe leather at the Salvation Army was fairly cheap. You could buy a pair of shoes for fifteen cents.
>
> This was a strange period in my life. Every time we finished work, we walked into a strange loneliness, a terrible loneliness. There is no greater loneliness than being in a crowd of people you don't know. The laundry girls and I lived in a profound, collective poverty.
>
> It was as if Charles Street did not exist for the rest of the people in the city. You even had difficulty getting a priest to come with the Eucharist. (They were afraid of the stevedores getting drunk.) They did bring the Eucharist,

but that's about all they came for. The church was very far away from us, even though geographically it was near. Nothing seemed to make too much sense on Charles Street. I guess when you live six in a little room and three in a bed, nothing much does make sense.

The ghost of starvation was always at my heels. When once you have really starved, you never really forget it. I don't mean the simple hunger people sometimes experience when they say, 'I could eat a horse!' No. I mean the starvation of people who are so weak from not eating that they can't lift a finger. That ghost of starvation lived somewhere in me. I don't know exactly where it lived, but when ever I was hungry, it rose to the surface. It rose up and seemed to laugh. The ghost of starvation laughing! Hunger laughing! But that's how it felt sometimes.

In bed we at least had warm quilts. We talked mostly about food! The girls would remark, 'Look, my belt is down one notch. I must be reducing.' One very thin girl already had a tiny waist. She was still losing weight because she was hungry. Seven dollars a week didn't come anywhere near to feeding us. We used to talk sometimes about 'sniffing' the food of the rich people and would go to Fifth Avenue with its big restaurants and walk through the alleys smelling the good food. Then we would come home and talk about it.

Events seem to dovetail in my life. Here were two kinds of starvations. The starvation I experienced in Russia was acceptable because everybody was starving. The hunger here in New York was harder to accept because here only a few were hungry — and not much was being done about it.

The temptation to give way to prostitution was always there:

The great temptation for a very hungry working girl in her early 20s was sex. I think there are a lot of saints in the slums. I don't think God would have been upset if any of those girls had gone with those men. The hunger was extreme. We worked long hours and ate meagerly.

One day when Catherine was working busily in Macy's Department Store, she met a certain Miss La Delle, who addressed her as Baroness and invited her to a meal in her home. Miss La Delle was one of those responsible for the 'Chautauqua',

23

a group of Protestant artists and educators who met at Chautauqua, New York, with a view to bringing culture and education to people living in the rural parts of Canada and the United States. This they did by shows, theatrical performances, music and lectures.

Catherine accepted the offer, and travelled around the whole of the United States with the group. She began earning quite a lot of money, most of which she spent on her son's education. She sent some to Boris, and some to her mother, who was living in exile in Belgium.

Catherine began to be famous. Her stories about Russia astonished and disturbed more and more people. (She got into difficulties with the Soviet Embassy's Secret Service, which considered her outspoken criticism of the Communist regime in Russia as dangerous.) During the performance in Halifax, she was contacted by the famous Leigh-Emmerich Lecture Bureau which promptly offered her $300 for each of her lectures. She also lectured about the poverty in America.

It was during this time of her public appearances that her talent, sparkling wit, charm and attractiveness often resulted in proposals of marriage. In the meantime, difficulties and tensions had arisen in her own married life. A great weariness was beginning to press in upon her, a weariness which had aleady begun at the age of fifteen, when she was first married. Then came the war years, the persecution, a wandering life, the experience of starvation and poverty. She was already tired.

One day, in New York, Father Edmund Walsh, SJ, who was responsible for the Near East Welfare Association, asked her to give lectures on behalf of the Catholic Arabs and other refugees. She accepted, and a spacious office was put at her disposal; she had more and more interesting and fascinating contacts. She was invited to parties and visited the luxurious and magnificent homes of the rich and the intelligentsia. Again, men ran after this blonde Russian, but it only annoyed her.

> During those days I was in the throes of hearing the Lord say, 'Sell what you possess. . . come follow me', and I was running away from him.

Catherine began to wonder more and more if God had saved her from death in Russia in order to make her rich and self-sufficient in North America. She was pursued by an irresistible urge to give away all she had earned in the last few years and

24

go and live among the poor in the slums. She prayed, fasted and sought advice.

It was 1929, when a great economic crisis was sweeping over the whole of the Western world.

In the poor quarter

As a child in school in Alexandria, Egypt, Catherine heard a Sister talk about St Francis of Assisi. She was so fascinated by the description of the saint that she cried out, 'One day I shall live as he did, among the poor'.

She often questioned her parents about being rich, and her father told her: 'God has given us a lot of money so that we can give it away to other people.' Catherine thought this was a very sensible answer. At home, she often gave away things she was fond of, and her parents often discovered that missing household articles had been given away by their dear daughter!

The idea of living in poverty disappeared for a time while she was married to Boris, but the horrors of war, and their subsequent flight, brought her back to the world of privation and suffering:

> In Finland and America that dream was a reality, but it wasn't my dream! It was as if somebody had thrust it upon me. It was someone else's dream. As I have already related, I was very poor, earning only seven dollars a week. I lived with the poor and was shocked to discover that in the richest country of the world there were terribly, terribly poor people. The Russian in me understood that I was one of the 'humiliati' as far as my new country was concerned. I was a foreigner, a nobody.
>
> This poverty of being a non-person was a kind of poverty that I had never expected to face in my wildest imagination. Many people in many countries experience this poverty, and it is a very, very hard kind to take. Yet, at that moment I realised that I was a non-person, the original dream came back. I realised that I was poor. I realised that what I had said and dreamt as a child in Ramleh was taking place. There was no statue of St Francis here, no birds, but I was poor. In fact, I was destitute.
>
> But there was in my heart and in that dream a rejoicing, and yet something was missing. The 'missing link' was my consent to it. I was poor in those early years because

25

circumstances made me poor. I didn't go and become poor myself. It wasn't a complete offering to God. It was an acceptance of God's will, yet accompanied by the desire to get out from under it.

Yes, this was something quiet different. I realized then that my dream was not being fulfilled in this way. I was just accepting the inevitable, and also accepting what I considered to be God's will and duty of the moment — but not too freely. There is a big difference.

Time marched on. I made good money, as a well-known celebrated lecturer. And when I was rich again the dream came back. It was now clear and sharp. It returned slowly, as I read the scriptures and thought about it. I wrote the fragments of the dream on all kinds of little pieces of paper. When I finally opened my purse one day, out came what I call the 'Little Mandate':

Arise — go! Sell all you possess. . . give it directly, personally to the poor. Take up My cross (their cross) and follow Me — going to the poor — being poor — being one with them — one with Me.

Little — be always little. . . simple — poor — childlike, Preach the Gospel! WITH YOUR LIFE WITHOUT COMPROMISE — listen to the Spirit — He will lead you. Do little things exceedingly well for the love of Me.

Love — love — love, never counting the cost.
Go into the marketplace and stay with me. . . pray. . . fast. . . pray. . . always. . . fast.

Be hidden — be a light to your neighbour's feet. Go without fear into the depths of men's hearts. . . I shall be with you.

Pray always. I WILL BE YOUR REST.

At this time in her life Catherine was well-off. With all this wealth she was indeed free to opt for poverty, but it took another three years before she was to put this dream into reality.

Her vocation took a decisive turn in spite of hesitations and difficulties. She consulted many priests (as she mentions in her autobiography), all of whom opposed her unusual longing. All of them said the same thing regarding her desire to go and live in the slums: 'You have a child, and your first duty is to take care of him.'

She then went to see Archbishop McNeil of Toronto. On a

previous occasion he had asked her to make an inquiry regarding the influence of communism in Toronto. Catherine completed the task and discovered that 28,000 Catholics had gone over to communism during the time of the great economic depression. She had given her information to the Episcopal Commission and to Fr Lamphier, who was in charge of the Catholic radio broadcasting. Thus, she was well known to the Archbishop.

She told him she was Polish and Russian, and had inherited from her Polish ancestors a great love for the Church. She wouldn't do anything without his permission. From her Rusian ancestors she inherited a desire to live the Gospel without compromise, and to go to the poor. She sked permission to sell all she possessed, except what was needed to provide for her son's education. She wanted to go and live in the slums of Toronto where, at this moment, people were starving; she wanted to live among them and serve them as an ordinary neighbour. It was that simple!

Archbishop McNeil asked her to wait a year, but to continue praying about it. After that he would 'cut the Gordian knot'.

During this extremely important and decisive time she moved, with her son George, into a pleasant and spacious flat on Isabella Street. When, a year later, the Archbishop finally gave his permission for her to put her dream into effect, she first made arrangements for her son's upbringing, gave him her Russian heirlooms, then sold everything else, together with the rest of her assets, and gave the money to the poor. On 15 October 1930 she left her luxurious flat and went to live in the slums.

> I remember the actual day very well. Carrying my suitcase and my spring-fall coat, I reached the room I rented a few days earlier. Inside there were only a few nails on which to hang my clothes, and a broken linoleum floor. It smelled of cabbage, just like all the other houses of the poor. Years later, on a festive Promise Day at Madonna House, I was to recall, in a poem, my first days in the slums of Toronto. Repeating here part of that poem is the best way I know of telling you what was in my heart that day:
>
> My hands were empty. I entered a small, drab house. The smell of poverty, cabbage and other cooking of the poor was in the air.
>
> A baby cried somewhere as I walked up a narrow stairway and entered the tiny room.

The window panes were grey with dust, so was the day outside. The single bed sagged in the middle. The two chairs were rickety, unsafe looking. The kitchen table scarred with ink and grease. The floor linoleum cracked in many places.

No cupboard for the few possessions that I had. Just nails with crumbling plaster on the wall.

Just nails. And a shelf or two. That is the room I came in. The room I knelt in that grey October day. Knelt and pledged my life to God forever and forever! There was no altar. Candles did not flicker. Neither did they sing their songs of flame, of love and death.

No priests were there to offer the Sacrifice for me. Nor was there any music, for there were no voices, young or old, to sing.

No altar linens, immaculate and freshly ironed by loving hands were there. But then, there was no altar to lay them on.

Nor was a table set anywhere for me. With beauty rare wrought by loving hands.

No. There was nothing of the sort. Just a poor, shabby room, and I kneeling on a cracked linoleum floor!

Yet, I would not exchange that day for any day today.

For well I know! My first promises were likewise my final ones. AND THERE WAS MUSIC IN THE AIR!!!

The cry of babies. The shout of children. The raucous cry of peddlers outside. The sound of traffic. Heavy traffic, that takes a shortcut through the slummy city streets. A woman calling to another across a back fence. The laughter of young people and a man.

All these blended for me. . . into a music of sheer ecstasy! There were to be 'my people'. In each my Love made love to me! It was Himself, who sang that day for me — the exquisite, incredible God-made melodies!

There was a priest in my gray room. The Lord of Hosts. Who is Himself Sacrifice and Victim! The altar? His altar was the world at my door. . . and the one He would make and bring me in the days to come! All of it was there — that day in my gray, shabby room.

There were tables set. One apart from me. Resplendent in beauty. Set not with man-made things, but God-made ones!

That day, I drank from His Cup of Love. And ate from Plates of Hope. My hands were filled with flowers of Faith. And Zeal shone a priceless necklace on my throat. . .

My ornate clothes were gone. I was bedecked in splendor! The gold of poverty shone like a thousand suns from them. The silver of Chastity made moonbeams pale! The jewels His love gave me in that gray room. . . on that gray October day — beggared the power of men's words!

The room became immense! And thousands of voices sang my wedding to the King!

I know His Mother was there, and she whose name I bear; the rest I could not see, blinded as I was with ecstasy!

Yes, I would not exchange my wedding day to God. . . in that gray shabby room. . . on that gray October day. . . for any day anywhere!

I praise His Name. . . My heart sings gratitude. . . even as angels sing before His throne, unceasingly!

For behold — the Pauper, who wedded me in a slummy stree, a crooked house, a shabby room. . . WAS A GREAT KING. . . CHRIST THE LORD. . . AND I BECAME THAT DAY A QUEEN. . . HIS SPOUSE! ALLELUIA! ALLELUIA! ALLELUIA!

As we listen to this account and witness of a beautiful, talented, and aristocratic woman, who because of Jesus gave away all she had and, in a radical way, went to live among the poor because she believed God was calling her to do it, we think of other conversion and vocation stories of saints who, in an analogous situation, surprised and shocked both the Church and world by their unconditional commitment and lifestyle. Whoever did such things during the economic and social crises of the 1930s could be sure of scandalising a lot of people, of being misunderstood, of being either hated or loved.

Life in the slums was unbelievably hard. Catherine spoke English with a slavic accent, and this became her passport to acceptance among the poor Polish and Ukrainian immigrants. She dressed poorly, and was living in the same circumstances as the other people in the neighbourhood. After paying her rent, and after she bought some food staples to stay alive, almost nothing was left of the money she had. It was then she started begging:

My food consisted of soup, tea, and old bread. Sometimes

there was no tea, just water. I confess very simply and humbly that I was continually hungry — there's no denying it. . .

The bed I slept on smelled from the use of many people; but then, the beds of the poor always smell. The sheets were rough. The blanket was very thin but I had my coat to keep me warm. I often wished I could get a hot water bottle someplace. But I decided that nobody else on Portland Street had a hot water bottle, so why should I? I didn't get one.

I had enough food to eat, but never enough to be completely filled. A beggar really cannot beg too much. Beggars must be humble; beggars cannot be choosers; beggars cannot, for instance, ask for a chocolate bar! It just isn't done. They can ask for cabbage, potatoes and carrots. But they cannot ask for butter. That's a luxury. Nor meat.

Catherine was searching for a new way of life, a new style of life. She simply wanted to live the life of a poustinik, a Russian hermit — praying, fasting, and working for the people. Very often she went to pray for a long time in the church next door. She made the way of the Cross, prayed the rosary, and often used prayers from the Eastern liturgy. But she preferred the direct prayer with God, the prayer of the heart.

She went regularly to visit the people, and kept an eye out for where she could be helpful in housekeeping, in service to the sick, the abandoned, the aged. Sometimes she stayed with people when they were ill, sleeping on the floor.

During this time of wrestling with herself, with doubts, and with God, she went to talk with Father Carr, her spiritual director. He suggested that from time to time she read a book on spirituality or theology. He gave her some lessons on dogma, moral theology, and the spiritual life, and she was sharing with him about Russian and Eastern spirituality.

He would say, 'We must read some books on the Byzantine Rite.' Then he would find a book on the Russian Fathers of the Desert at the Medieval Institute in Toronto. He would read and say, 'This is very good, very good. Is this what you've been telling me? It's an impossible way of life!' I would say, 'They lived it, why can't I?'

Friendship House

Catherine was hoping to live a Nazareth, hidden, type of life, and to identify, at the same time, with the poor. But this dream didn't last long. Her example and way of life attracted three women and two men to live the same way of life with her. This was the beginning of the Friendship House Apostolate which would have such a large influence in both Canada and the United States.

The result of this community forming around Catherine was that they had to find larger accommodations, and separate housing for the men and the women. But together they would take care of the desperate, the bitter, the lonely, in the poor quarter.

Food was still a big problem. Regularly they received some bread, vegetables and meat from a priest friend, Father Joseph Ferguson, who was working in the rural districts not far from Toronto. They distributed this to the hungry, living very sparsely themselves, and sometimes working sixteen to eighteen hours a day helping people.

> Periodically we gave away our bedding and slept on the floor in our overshoes and overcoats. Once I remember covering myself with a carpet.
>
> All this may appear heroic, but am not writing it to give that impression. I am just telling the truth so that future generations may know what the pioneers of Friendship House had to go through, and what the good Lord in his immense mercy and wisdom, taught us in his strange novitiate. . . One day, during one of my visits with Archbishop McNeil, he handed me a newspaper with a format of only four pages. It was called the *Catholic Worker*. He told me that the woman who was responsible for it, Dorothy Day, wrote as I spoke. He said that he would pay my fare to New York so I could meet her. I took advantage of his offer.
>
> It is difficult to describe my first meeting with Dorothy Day. In some ways it was historical, because Dorothy Day and I were pioneers in the lay apostolate. She had a wonderful influence on me. From our meeting a deep friendship was born which had, in a sense, profound repercussions on the whole lay apostolate of North America. I found Dorothy in a storefront very much like ours,

31

feeding a breadline in the same way we did — by prayer and begging. She was associated at the time with Peter Maurin, and she was publishing the *Catholic Worker*. She was just starting her 'House of Hospitality'.

She invited me to spend the night with her. I was to sleep with her in a double bed in a room that was filled with cots. People literally had to climb over one another to get to the beds near the walls. She was providing hospitality to women who were homeless due to the Depression. There were about 15 people in this one room.

As we were preparing for bed there was a knock on the door. A woman (definitely a woman of the streets) without a nose and with active syphilis, walked in and asked if we had a room for her.

Dorothy welcomed her like a queen and said, 'Of course we do.' Turning to me she said, 'I have a mattress, Catherine. I will put it in the huge bathtub, and you will be as snug as a bug in a rug. I will share the bed with this lady'.

Speaking as a nurse, I took Dorothy aside and warned her, 'This woman has active syphilis. Make sure you have no cuts on your body. You might easily contract the disease through a cut.' Then I received my first lesson from Dorothy. Usually so mild, gentle and kind, Dorothy suddenly arose and in a spirited voice said, 'Catherine, you have little faith. This is Christ come to us for a place to sleep. He will take care of me. You have to have faith!' This is one of the many lessons she was to teach me by her witnessing and by her example.

During this visit it was decided that Friendship House in Toronto would help promote the apostolate of the Catholic Worker. These two forms of apostolate would gradually grow together and would play a very important role in the concrete application of the social doctrine of the Church.

More and more people came to Toronto to visit Friendship House. Sociologists, guest lecturers, journalists, and the ever-present curiosity seekers. The famous French Catholic philosophers, Jacques Maritain and Etienne Gilson, also came to visit.

Catherine became involved in the struggle for labour unions, and to pressurise the government to create jobs. As a result she was often to give conferences. Once again she became famous! But difficulties and conflicts continued. Her way of speaking was forceful and direct. Especially when she was talking about justice, she wasn't afraid of anyone. She was criticised for being 'left wing'. Many priests were negative towards her. Suspicions swelled around her. At school, her son George was told that if he was really concerned with prospering later on in life, he and his mother should associate with a better class of people!

Catheine, who had once dreamt of a lonely, poustinik vocation was, all of a sudden, standing in the midst of an active and hectic apostolate, the target of gossip and criticism. The passion and way of the Cross of her mother as a refugee in Belgium, bcame hers also. When she went to find encouragement from the Archbishop, he simply pointed to the crucifix on the wall.

As the opposition and criticism grew, she decided to close Friendship House and leave Toronto. But the apostolate would continue; the flame was still aglow. From 1930-38 three houses had been founded in Canada — Toronto, Ottawa and Hamilton. From 1938-46 the work would continue to flourish in the United States — Harlem, Chicago, Shreveport, Los Angeles, Portland, Oregon, Marathon, Wisconsin, and Washington, DC

Catherine has written some very remarkable meditations and poems about her Toronto adventure or experiment in which can be seen the extent to which her faith in Jesus and in her vocation was tested and purified — but not destroyed.

She was advised to go and stay for a while with Dorothy Day in New York. Dorothy was waiting for her at Central Station. She brought her to the Catholic Worker and when Catherine came in she was welcomed by Dorothy's co-workers with the hymn 'Iste Confessor', the hymn sung in the liturgy for a confessor of the faith!

Catherine stayed with them for a few days. She was then invited by the publisher of the *Catholic Sign* magazine, Father Theophane McGuire, to take on a special assignment. He proposed that she go to Europe and write a series of articles on Catholic Action and the Lay Apostolate. She accepted. It was the year 1937.

Europe
Portugal was the first country Catherine visited. She met Salazar and had a long conversation with him. Then she travelled with

another woman to visit Fatima. She made many contacts with lay people active in rural apostolates.

She went to Salamanca in Spain to report on the Falangist movement. The civil war was at its height. Franco had his headquarters in Salamanca, and most of the Spanish cardinals and bishops were there as well. Catherine grasped the situation very quickly. She saw that many prelates and important people had neglected to put the social teaching of the Church into practice. On the other hand, many poor parish priests, monasteries and convents were spared by the communists because they were helping the poor.

She wrote many touchy articles and reports about this lack of application of the social doctrine of the Church in Spain, but those articles were never published by *Sign*.

Together with a correspondent from the *New York Times* she received permission to travel to Brunette, a town on the French border, which had been recaptured by the communists. They entered the church. Consecrated hosts were profaned by having been inserted in faeces. In the nearby cemetery of a Carmelite monastery they saw disinterred bodies of monks and nuns, naked and arranged in positions of sexual intercourse. They went to a hospital where the Carmelite Sisters were nursing. They were allowed to visit a twenty-year-old nun who had been raped by fifteen soldiers. After she had been raped they cut off her breasts and cut her thighs up in small pieces. She was dying. As a result of seeing such tragedies, Catherine fainted.

She couldn't stay any longer in Spain, and decided to go to France. The border security was very tight. She was told to strip naked, and a female doctor came and examined literally everything, looking for gold being smuggled across the border. Humiliated, and hurt by all she had seen in such a short time in this broken country, she took the train to Paris to gather information on Catholic action.

Catherine was always intensely interested in social action. As much as possible she tried to contact the labour movements, the cooperatives, the trade unions and other social organisations. As soon as she arrived in Paris she went to see the Little Brothers of the Poor. They were busy taking care of the aged, the sick, and the lonely, what we call today the 'Fourth World'.

She met also the Companions of St Francis, a group of dramatists who were performing in the public streets and squares. Their plays concerned the social situation and the cry for more justice. She met a certain Father Dominic, a Dominican, who was the pastor of a Russian Catholic church. She attended a meeting with the great Russian philosopher Berdyaev, and Jacques and Raissa Maritain. She met the famous Emmanuel Mounier, author of *A Personalist Manifesto*, and editor of the new journal, *Esprit*. These contacts would enrich and influence her views on her vocation and service to the Church.

She met the Dominican publishers, Cerf, and the members of La Pierre Qui Vivre, a retreat house outside of Paris. (Many years later Cerf would publish the French edition of *Poustinia*.)

Paris too had its slums encircling the city. Catherine applied for a fifty-day work permit and went to live in what was called the red belt district of Paris. She found a job in a candy shop. During tea-time she went into the poor areas to chat with the young workers in the pubs not far from her place of work. Her stay in Paris was a success. She collected a great deal of information about the lay apostolate and the actual needs of the Church there.

Then she went to Belgium where her mother and younger brother Andrew were living. Here also she tried to contact Catholic action organisations. She attended meetings and activities of various youth groups, especially those composed of middle-class university students. She was very impressed by the Young Christian Workers, and met the founder, Abbé (later Cardinal) Cardijn. She was especially impressed by their days of recollection, and the realistic approach they took to the social questions of the day.

When she returned to New York, her conversations with Father Theophane about France weren't too hopeful:

> I based my opinion on what I had learned in the 'red belt'. The world was heading for a major catastrophe, but the priests were bourgeois, with just enough education to separate them from reality. In most of the movements something was lacking — real honest-to-goodness *action*. There were too many discussions, just too much talking. It made me tired. I imagined that the Lord himself would walk away from those endless discussions.

'Katie', as she was often called in the States, kept her own direct style of speaking and acting, and this scandalised many people.

In July, 1939, she was again sent to Europe by *Sign* to find out how Catholics were faring in Poland, which was at war with Germany. In September of that year she was in Warsaw where the war was raging violently. The Stukas whined ceaselessly overhead. All the able-bodied men had left the city and Warsaw was filled with women, children, and old people. She saw once again the cruelty of war which she had seen in Russia and Spain. Once again she saw crippled bodies, corpses, distress and misery.

> I remember sleeping on the floor of a large hotel. . . I only had a back pack, the old-fashioned kind you carry like a baby, with pajamas and some bread inside. Inside the bread I carried a Retina 11 camera. I photographed the women digging the trenches, the hospital table in the middle of the street, the children, the destruction of Warsaw.

With a group of journalists and many refugees they marched along the railway in the direction of Hungary. But this route was also being watched by the Stukas. Regular bombardments followed, and once again Catherine was in the middle of distress, sadness and the misery of people who were fleeing for their lives.

> When we arrived in the Carpathian mountains in Czechoslovakia, it began to rain. What a sight we were! People of all ages, pregnant women, wounded soldiers, all refugees from this Polish holocaust, all oppressed in their souls by this calamity. How different life becomes when you have to flee to preserve it!

After one week of struggling and marching they arrived at the Hungarian border where they were picked up and put on a train for Budapest. There she met her cousin Nicholas Makletzoff, who was also a refugee from Russia. They left together for Italy, travelled to France, and from there back to the States.

Shortly afterwards she was invited by Father John Lafarge, SJ and Cardinal Hayes to live in Harlem. With a few clothes in a small handbag, she set out to begin a new Friendship House.

Harlem

> My room in Harlem had the same kind of patched linoleum floor as my little room in Toronto. I used to lie on the linoleum and cry out to God; 'Why have you brought me here? Why have you asked me to try to bring racial justice

36

to a land born from a revolution for justice?' I couldn't undestand these contradictions. I was all mixed up. Truth and untruth — all mixed together. The United States had this marvelous Constitution, but it didn't apply to Negroes. The pursuit of happiness! For whom? Whites only.

Thus she wrote about her new adventure to Harlem. The racial apartheid, which was a real problem at that time in the United States, would make it difficult for Catherine's work and witness. In this new Friendship House, Catherine had the feeling of lying between two enemy trenches, with the guns blazing over her. In many of the Catholic schools and churches there was real apartheid. It made her very sad.

This was hypocrisy. Where was God in it all! I used to spend nights praying on my linoleum floor in Harlem. Yes, Russia too was sinful. We had our pogroms. The Jews were the Tsar's scapegoats whenever anything went wrong. But these were nothing compared to what I saw in America.

Once again she started lecturing and giving conferences in which she proclaimed loudly that blacks, Puerto Ricans, Poles, Ukrainians, and so many other immigrants, were also human beings. White Americans considered themselves superior, but they should, on the contrary, respect and love these people.

One day she was lecturing in the south in Savannah, Georgia. Men and women rushed on to the stage and started attacking her physically. She received blows to the face and her dress was torn. One day, in Friendship House, Harlem, a man walked in and spat in her face: 'That's for you, you white-blooded nigger lover.'

Catherine also lectured to nuns and priests. She insisted they should also take black children into their schools. Most of the time her message was unwelcome. She was told she was hopelessly naive, and that the time was not yet ripe. In the meantime, black mothers and fathers came to see her and asked her to intervene, in order that their children would be admitted to white schools, or so that they would be considered in their parishes as equal Christians.

Catherine went to see the school principals and the parish priests. If this didn't help, she asked Cardinal Spellman to intervene on behalf of her beloved black brothers and sisters. The black population became restless and began to react.

America got nervous. People panicked and became frightened because the situation got worse and worse. But Cardinal Spellman of New York, and Cardinal Stritch of Chicago, both asked her to continue speaking and promoting racial justice. Her apostolate was growing in New York, as well as in other major cities: Chicago, Washington, DC, and Portland, Oregon. Her new Friendship House in Harlem became more and more famous in the Church in America. Not everyone was positive about Catherine. Thus, in Harlem as in Toronto, lack of understanding and respect were her constant companions.

One day she was invited as a guest speaker to Fordham University in New York. In private conversation with her, the Jesuits who ran the university would not accept her arguments about accepting black students. Finally, they invited her to address the students themselves:

> I came to talk to you, not to lecture. In ten minutes I am stepping off this platform. Ten minutes is no lecture, as far as I am concerned. The situation here is very tragic. You have a chapel in this building, and there is a crucifix in the chapel. This same cross shines all over New York. However, the words of the Person who died on that cross are ignored in these holy precincts. According to your teachers, the administration has turned thumbs down on the admittance of a Negro boy. They told me that you do not want undergraduate Negroes. That's why I am getting down off this platform right now.

'Don't go', they shouted, 'talk to us, talk to us! Catherine then gave them one of the most impressive talks of her life about racial justice, about blacks and other marginal groups in society. Then someone got up and asked for a show of hands on whether or not they were going to accept blacks in the school. There were unanimous cries of 'Yes, yes!' 'Thank you', said Catherine, 'God is happy tonight'.

But the Jesuits were not happy with her performance at all. She was invited again to meet with some twenty of the priests alone.

> 'Baroness,' one of them began, 'you realize, don't you, that many of our students are from the South. If we accept a Negro, there will be a great hullabaloo among the parents and the students.'

I said, 'Oh, excuse me, Father, I thought you were teaching Christianity here.' There was a dead silence. I continued, 'I have a little Gospel book here. I would like to read something that I think fits this situation.'

Nobody asked me to read it.

Another priest began: 'Baroness, we have to move slowly. The time is not yet ripe.'

I said, 'Is that so, Father? I have never read anywhere in the Gospel where Christ says to wait 20 years before living the Gospel. The Good News is for now. He died for all men, to make all men his brothers and sisters, children of his Father. He didn't advocate brotherhood in 20 years or 100 years. He expects it to be *now*. He said, "Go and preach the Gospel" and he means it. Have you ever read the Gospel from that point of view, Father?'

It was someone else's turn. 'But we will go broke!' I said: 'It's a question of what you're more interested in, God or Mammon. God said you cannot serve two masters.'

For almost two hours they badgered me with objections, and I refuted them as best I could. Their great temptation was to compromise with the Gospel. The last sentence I remember saying was, 'Fathers, please don't ask me any more. I love you very much. Your Founder has been a big influence in my own life. A Jesuit guided me spiritually when I was only twelve years old and living in Egypt. Don't break my heart. What you are doing is compromising with the Gospel. Ignatius of Loyola would never do that.'

Thomas Merton, in his autobiography, *The Seven-Storey Mountain*, also wrote about Catherine's struggle for justice, and her radical interpretation of the Gospel in the harlems of poverty and discrimination. She had just finished her lecture in the auditorium of St Bonaventure's University in Orlean, New York. As he walked in she was answering questions forcefully and directly. 'This must be the Baroness', Merton remarked.

Indeed it was. Afterwards Merton met her on several other occasions. He struggled with the choice between joining her work in Harlem, or joining the Trappists. Both were the radical Gospel for which his soul was was thirsting. After spending several months in Harlem, he decided on the Trappists. Catherine and Merton continued to correspond until his death. While in Harlem he discovered that the secret of her success was that she didn't rely on fragile human methods and techniques, but on the power of Christ and his Holy Spirit. Catherine thus had a real influence on Merton's vocation.

More and more people were talking about Catherine in the American Church and asking for her assistance. During World War II she was asked by the bishops to make a survey of Christian life among the young, and among those working in factories. She went incognito and worked as a bar maid, getting to know the workers and asking questions about the faith. Some years later she published a rather shocking book called *Dear Bishop*. They were letters from 'Katie' to the Bishop who was living far away from his people in his beautiful bishop's house. She wrote about cocktail girls and the ordinary people she had met in the bars and factories. 'Katie' was a fictitious person in the book, but what she told the bishops was rough and stark reality. She was familiar with this reality, because she had been living in it since 1921, when she had been deprived of everything and was part of it.

Friendship House, Harlem, was situated on 138th Street. Here was Catherine's famous small room with the linoleum floor. There were also several establishments on both sides of 135th Street — a lending library, a clothing room, and a place for socialising.

The Friendship Houses in the United States which stemmed from Harlem had a familiar (but not formal) relationship with the Catholic Worker houses founded by Dorothy Day. They were both contemporary forms of evangelisation among the poor in rich countries. With these poor Catherine and her followers sought to identify, to become one with, by living with them 'in the heart of the masses'. Thus was she attempting to fulfil the mission which Jesus had entrusted to her — to live the Gospel, and to proclaim the Gospel without compromise.

Living among the poor, Catherine used what she called the 'chit-chat' apostolate from the beginning. Every day she walked from her flat on 138th Street, along Lennox Avenue to the library, and then to the flat on 135th Street. There were many little shops along the way, and Catherine would stop and chat with people as they opened their shops, swept the sidewalks, or cleaned the windows for the day's business. With her rough Slavic accent they knew she was Russian, knew she was on their side in the struggle for social justice. More importantly, they also knew she was a woman of faith and prayer.

Little by little she got to know her new friends. Many of the people in her chit-chat apostolate came to see her and, since the other members of Friendship House used the same method, the number of visitors increased. There was a warehouse for second-hand clothing. From here they brought the clothing to the homes of the needy and so, in still another way, they came into contact with the people, listening to them and encouraging them.

> How many realities of their lives were revealed to us over these cups of coffee! How much sorrow, pain, worry and even a few little joys were told to us in friendship over a kitchen table which often had a fourth leg propped up with bricks. Conversations like that are the essence of any life of love, and always will be. They were the core and essence of Friendship House, and they are of Madonna House today.

For Catherine, identification with the poor meant that she wanted to live among the poor in the same conditions and share the same way of life:

> It would have been impossible to identify ourselves with the Negroes in Harlem if we had not lived in Harlem. We had to be poor as they were poor. We had to experience the way of life they experienced; the crowded apartments with their poor ventilation; unbearably hot in the summer and unbearably cold in the winter. We had to experience the poor plumbing which, at times, could threaten our very lives. . .
> Because we identified in these ways, those who received things from us did not hate us. They began to love us. The law of love, the law of Christ, began to work in Harlem in a tangible way. This was the cement of the whole structure of love, of the whole apostolate. Such cement is not easy to make. Its source is God, and prayer was the channel through which it came to us from him.

Every day Catherine and her staff assisted at the 7.00 a.m. Mass at the neigbouring parish of St Mark's. After breakfast they came together for Prime and Lauds before work. After lunch they returned to St Mark's for spiritual reading, a visit to the Blessed Sacrament, and to pray the rosary. After supper they prayed Evening Vespers. Besides this communal prayer they also spent time in private prayer. As far as possible, they followed this daily prayer schedule between 6.30 a.m. and 11 p.m. every day. They were constantly overwhelmed by the many problems and the work to be done in the neighbourhood. Once a year they made a retreat of three days and had a monthly day of recollection. Cardinal Spellman suggested that they also have a few weeks' vacation every year. They begged the money for this since it was not part of their budget!

From time to time, during these years, Catherine would go to a small village in Canada called Combermere, where her cousin Nicholas had built a small fishing cabin. It is now the centre of her whole apostolate.

The need for money was constant and very pressing. They were always on the look-out for new ways and means of raising money to answer the needs of the people.

One day a Russian refugee came to see Catherine:

> Kossoff was tall and very handsome, a Rudolph Valentino type, with a beard and all.
>
> He said to me, 'Catherine, I haven't any money.' I answered 'Neither have I.'
>
> He said, 'How would you like to dance the tango with me and make some money?' I said, 'Sure, let's try.' We went to Greenwich Village. I wore an evening gown and he wore a tuxedo. We started dancing together in a cocktail lounge and were quite successful. A collection was taken up afterwards and we made ten dollars.
>
> My God that was a lot of money! So we went into this dance routine in a very big way and started to become quite popular.

All the while Catherine kept on arguing, pleading for equal rights for the black people in Harlem and the United States.

> To lecture about the Negro was to take your life in your hands. Once I lectured in Flatbush. Do you know what was thrown at me there? A cabbage! Have you ever been hit by a cabbage?
>
> It struck me right on the temple, and I fell down. You could call me a confessor of the faith struck down by a cabbage! Some people are wounded with knives. Others are pelted with stones or with something equally exciting. Me, I get hit with a cabbage!
>
> Living in Harlem was both heaven and hell. The hell

had been created by men, the heaven by God. Even to this day, my heart smiles at the sight of a Negro face, because to me it is like an icon of Christ. I was so at home in Harlem, so at home.

Difficulties and problems began to arise among the members of Friendship House. There were tensions, misunderstandings and disagreements as to the direction Friendship House should take in its apostolic endeavours. Catherine was saddened by these conflicts.

One day a man walked into the library. 'My name is Eddie Doherty, and this is my assistant. We've been assigned', he said, 'to write an article for *Liberty* magazine about the wickedest city in the world — Harlem.' Catherine exploded. 'Why don't you write about how people like you made it the wickedest city in the world!' All her negative feelings about haughty white Americans welled up within her.

Eddie pointed to his secretary and said that she told him Catherine Doherty was the only person who could give him an authentic picture of Harlem. 'Why don't you write an article, "Harlem, the Saintliest City in the World?" After all, these people are under your heel and still they survive, they pray, and go to church. I don't see any reason for writing the kind of article you have in mind.'

He said, 'I'll be back.' He did come back and kept coming back. He became a regular visitor to Friendship House. Once in a while he and Catherine went out for walks together. Ostensibly he was asking her for information about Harlem; actually he was gathering information for a book on *her* life! He found *her* more fascinating than Friendship House!

Their relationship improved. Catherine started paying more and more attention to his life and work. At that time, Eddie Doherty was one of the best known journalists in America. Besides articles and reviews, he had written books, texts for radio programmes, and even scripts for motion pictures. His book about her life — *Tumbleweed* — was the result of their many conversations during their walks and dinners together.

They fell in love. After doing the script in Hollywood for the film, 'The Sullivan Brothers', Eddie came to see Catherine. At that time she was staying in Friendship House, Chicago. He asked her to go with him to see the Bishop about their relationship. The Bishop at first thought it impossible for Eddie to marry Catherine. He was too rich; his salary was too high. If he really wanted to marry her he would have to give first priority for her work with Friendship House. Eddie said he was willing to do that because he really loved her. The Bishop said he could go on writing, but she would continue to live on begging, in keeping with her vocation from God.

Thus, on 25 June 1943, they were married by the Bishop in his chapel at St Andrew's Parish, Chicago. The reaction of the other members of the apostolate was sharp. But when they heard that Eddie was willing to give away his possessions, they accepted and agreed.

Eddie had been widowed twice, and had two sons. He and Catherine went to live in a small apartment in Chicago. He proved to be a companion full of understanding and compassion.

The growing internal tensions in the apostolate had broken down Catherine's resistance and undermined her health. At a convention in Chicago in 1946 the Friendship House members rejected her ideas and vision for the apostolate. So, in 1947, she and Eddie left for Canada, where they had been invited by Bishop Smith of the Pembroke diocese to work with the poor in the rural areas. Bishop Sheil gave them his car for the trip, filled with books and personal belongings. They drove to Combermere. 'As we drove. . . I remember experiencing a fantastic sweetness. It was as if God had kissed me, and his face was black.'

On 17 May 1947 Catherine and Eddie arrived in Combermere without any support. On the day of arrival, still reeling from all that had happened, they planted some apple trees. They began their new life in a little white house on the banks of the Madawaska River. It was a new period in the life of the Church. It was the beginning of the Madonna House Apostolate.

A new adventure

Combermere was well known to Catherine from the late twenties and early thirties. Almost every year she had come to Ottawa Valley to relax and take a holiday. She knew many people in the area. This would be a great help to her in the early days because the first few months in this beautiful but harsh land were not easy. Once again she had to enter into poverty and the struggle to survive. She was moving from the big cities of New York, Chicago and Toronto to the isolation of the Canadian hinterland where the local inhabitants had to stand shoulder to shoulder to survive.

The climate in the Madawaska Valley is not mild. The long and cold winters make life hard and taxing. There was no electricity. The house was heated by a wood furnace, and wood was regularly procured from the forest. There was a well in the basement from which they obtained their water, and there was a hand-pump in the house. Catherine built an outdoor toilet, and went to the river to wash clothes. She lived with Eddie and another woman, Grace Flewelling, an old and dear friend who had been with Catherine in the apostolate for many years.

They rose around 5.30 a.m. to start the bread, fill the stove with wood, put on the water kettle, and make the porridge. If there was a priest, they went to the little parish church for Mass. If there was no priest they prayed Lauds until breakfast. During spring and summer Catherine worked in the garden.

There were always the meals to prepare. After lunch they usually went to the church for adoration, and took some time for spiritual reading. The afternoons were devoted to letter writing and arranging the library. Gradually food and clothes began coming in for the poor; Catherine had to provide space for these donations. After supper and the dishes they prayed the rosary and said evening prayer.

And so the new Nazareth life of the Baroness began to take shape. There were many contacts with the local people and many friends from former times sent support and encouragement. New candidates arrived. In Combermere, this small, rustic village hidden among rivers and valleys and woods, Catherine was discovering something of her Russian nature. Memories of her roots and origins were now of great help to her.

From her mother she had learned to do all kinds of manual work and housekeeping. She could wash and cook and sew. But most of all she had learned from her parents how to care for the poor and those less fortunate than herself:

> Upon the death of my father, my mother found among his books one which she had never seen before. On the flyleaf was written: 'My debt to God.' He listed the things he considered his debt to God. He had sponsored many people through college. He had an interest in what today are called 'detox' centres. He gave dowries, like St Nicholas, to girls who couldn't marry because they were too poor. Yes, the list of Father's 'debt to God' was rather long.
>
> I thought all parents were like mine, but now I know

better. Not for a moment did they ever neglect to instill Gospel attitudes in me. In my organisation of the apostolate, I used the ideas and patterns I had learned from my parents. In my books I describe this spirituality of Madonna House, and how the ideas and inspirations of my parents took on flesh in Combermere over the years.

Some events in the early days had a special influence on later developments. Catherine had decided to start a summer programme in Combermere which would offer courses on the lay apostolate and Catholic action. She was looking for lecturers to give the conference. Father Eugene Cullinane was the superior of the Basilian Fathers in Rochester, New York, and also the principal of Aquinas Institute, a school with 1,700 students. He was still a seminarian in Toronto when he first met Catherine. She wrote to him and asked him to help her organise the 1950 seminar. He accepted. But a few weeks later something came up and he was unable to come. He proposed to send another priest in his place, Father John Callahan, who was very active in the Catholic Action movement. Father Callahan came for the summer seminar in July 1950. He was destined to become the first priest of Madonna House and the Director General of all future priests.

In April 1951 Father Callahan returned to give the annual retreat to the budding community. He became ill. The doctor advised him to rest for several months. He asked if he could rest here in Combermere. It was during this time that he discovered within himself a desire to join Catherine's apostolate as a priest, with the permission of his bishop.

Catherine was overjoyed! She had never dared to even dream that priests would come and join her. Shortly after Father Callahan's arrival, other priests came to join: Father Emile Briere, Father Cullinane himself, and Father Paul Bechard. In the years to follow, five men would be ordained priests from the community — Fathers Bob Pelton, Richard Starks, Thomas Zoeller, David May and Ron Cafeo. Priests would play a very important part in the development of Madonna House, presiding over the Eucharist and the life of prayer, and particularly as spiritual directors for the members of the community.

In 1951 Catherine went to Rome to attend the International Lay Congress as the official representative of Bishop Smith of Pembroke. The Bishop had given her an official letter of recommendation for Cardinal Montini, then Secretary of State and the future Pope Paul VI. The Cardinal arranged a personal interview for her with Pope Pius XII. Then, on 14 October, the Cardinal had a long talk with Catherine during which he presented her with a new proposal. He asked her to consider becoming a secular institute of Pontifical rite according to the new directives of Provida Mater Ecclesia, Pius XII's recent instruction on secular Institutes. The members of Friendship House would remain lay, but be permanently joined to the Church by the three evangelical promises of poverty, chastity and obedience. Catherine reported this to Bishop Smith, and wrote to Betty Schneider, who at that time was the national director of the Friendship Houses in the States.

After discussion, the members of the Friendship Houses in the United States rejected the proposal. They were afraid they would lose ther lay character and become some kind of religious order. The Canadian members accepted the proposal, seventeen voting for and only one against. The name of the Friendship House in Canada was changed to Madonna House. In 1955 Catherine and her husband Eddie made their promise to live a celibate life. In 1969, Eddie was ordained a priest in the Melkite rite in Nazareth by Monsignor Joseph Raya, the Archbishop of Galilee. In later years Archbishop Raya would come to retire at Madonna House and become a full member of the community. Father Eddie died on 4 May 1975.

In 1956 a constitution of Madonna House seeking secular institute status was approved by Bishop Smith. It was sent to Rome. As no answer came from Rome for a long time the Bishop inquired as to the reason. He was informed that Madonna House could not become a secular institute as long as men and women were living in one community of prayer and work. Men and women were living, of course, in separate quarters, but they were eating and praying and working together. This mixed aspect of their life they considered essential, and didn't wish to lose it.

To avoid this complication it was decided to apply for Pious Union status under the local Bishop, rather than that of a secular institute.

Bishop Smith approved Madonna House as a Pious Union on 8 June 1960. The women's branch was called Domus Dominae, the House of Our Lady, and the laymen's and priests' branch was called Domus Domini, the House of the Lord. Although canonically two branches, the common way of life remained unchanged.

On the same day of his approval, Bishop Smith came to bless Madonna House and the new bronze statue of Our Lady of Combermere. The original title of the statue (by Frances Rich of California) was 'The Questing Madonna'. Our Lady is a beautiful woman with her arms outstretched over the Madawaska Valley. She is both protecting Madonna House and welcoming the pilgrims who come to her house. The statue has a very special place in the heart of Catherine and in the heart of the whole community which bears her name.

Fulfilment of a vocation
During the 1960s and 1970s many, many men and women would visit Madonna House; priests, sisters, and even bishops would come. Some of the young people would ask to become members, choosing Madonna House as a lifetime vocation. During the early years of 1970 Catherine would put the finishing touches to the official Constitution of Madonna House. Her spirituality was deepening all the time and taking on a definite form. She herself was busy during the last twenty-five years of her life, writing, giving speeches and conferences, talking personally to people. All this was rooted ever more deeply in the heart of the Church.

The first poustinia was opened in 1962. It was fixed up to become a place for prayer, solitude and fasting. The 1960s were full of problems, doubts, anxieties and confusion. These pent-up feelings often exploded in Madonna House. Many religious and priests were struggling with their 'identity', and the hippies and 'revolutionaries' were fighting for their causes. All came to see and talk with Catherine.

> Thus, when the renewal hit the religious orders, people by the thousands began to come to Combermere to see men and women living in chastity. While nuns were jumping over the walls and priests were getting married, a group of people lived peacefully (comparatively speaking!), attending to its business. Some priests joined us. In a sense, God seemed to be walking several steps ahead of events through me, and presenting our community as some kind of model.
>
> Walking out of a meeting at the University of Toronto, I came upon a group of hippies, sleeping and lying on the grass. One girl stopped me and asked, 'Are you a nun without a habit?' (She had seen my silver cross shining in the sun.) I said, 'No, I'm a person'. . .

For 10 days, four hours a day — first 40, then 50, then 100, then 200 hippies — I talked to them about Teresa of Avila, Francis of Assisi, St John of the Cross. I read to them from Francis Thompson's Hound of Heaven. I spoke to them of the Russian saints, the Desert Fathers, and Elizabeth of the Trinity.

They had found a guru. Many of them travelled to Combermere where they were welcomed, but it was not an easy time. Catherine thought they had a right to know the truth of the Gospel, and to enjoy the warmth and hospitality of Christian love. They didn't forget their tribulations on campus, but they got some new perspectives.

Thus the new trends in philosophy and theology, and the sudden changes in the Church and the world swept over Combermere. The 'God is dead' theology invaded the community. It was a strange and frightening time. The community became a sounding-board for what was going on among the young priests and nuns and all the confused and frustrated people.

In the early sixties, the Church appeared to be in chaos, to be going over some kind of precipice. It seemed to be dissolving. But I knew, with a faith that nothing could shake, that the powers of hell would never prevail. Nothing seemed to affect my faith, the powerful faith that God had given me. It became a sort of pivot around which young people began to gather. Something of the deep faith that God had endowed me with penetrated those hippies, those young people. Faith in the Church, faith in the Lord, faith in Our Lady. I discerned in my soul that this was the moment of faith.

Catherine thought very much of Our Lady in those days, of the swords that had pierced her heart. They were swords of distress, and Mary was once again carrying the body of her dead son in her lap. Catherine kept on advising her staff to make Madonna House a centre where the hospitality of the gospel is practised, and where, with open heart and mind, one does not flee the reality of a changing Church and world.

She regularly wrote articles and poems and books to communicate her thoughts and ideas. Her specal concern was for priests. All her life she had had a special love for priests, and now that love was needed more than ever. They were going through an identity crisis. She listened to them, helped them through endless discussions about structures, celibacy and apostolate. She helped them to discover their own sense of priesthood. She did it in her own way — with much human warmth, but not neglecting her own direct and surprising approach! She possessed the secret of approaching people, touching them with the flame of her own convictions, her immense faith, and her burning mystical love for God.

> I don't know how many priests remained in the priesthood because of Madonna House. Maybe our own priests could tell me. All I know is that in talking to me I represented something to them, and they knew that I loved them. They confided in me, asked my advice, discussed with me their most intimate personal problems. Many remained in the priesthood. They remained because Madonna House was there, stood firm, unshakable in its faith in God and in the Church. Their letters to me bear witness to what happened to them. . .
>
> Hour after hour, day in and day out, I told them: 'Please, give us the Eucharist, give us sacraments, give us the word of God. We need you. We lay people can be the psychiatrists, we can go to the inner city. We can do many things. But we cannot do your work. Be priests for us. Why do you want to be somebody else?'

Many nuns also came to speak with her. She was often invited to attend their chapters of renewal, and was present at more than eighteen such sessions. The talks and discussions centred mainly around interpreting their rules and constitutions in keeping with the new guidelines of Vatican II. She was often shocked and indignant upon hearing that, for many of them, renewal meant nothing more than how to get rid of their habits, use make-up, and take holidays.

Sometimes, at the end of these sessions, they asked Catherine to give the final speech. Those who know the way of life at Madonna House, or who have any knowledge about Catherine's views on poverty, will understand well the following passage:

> For accommodations I was given the 'cell' of one of the sisters. The 'cell' consisted of a 20 by 30-foot bedroom with an adjoining office, and next to the office a kitchenette,

equipped with all the latest electrical gadgets. Of course, the refrigerator was filled with snacks of all kinds. I couldn't sleep in that suite. All night long I was up and down, up and down. Finally, in the morning light, I found the chapel, not far from my 'cell'. I slept there. They all had 'cells' like that.

So I gave my talk. In the middle of it I suddenly put my head down on the lectern and began to cry. I sobbed and sobbed and sobbed. Then, feeling as if I had cords in my hands, I spoke. You have never heard such a lecture!

Afterwards the chaplain called me into his office and said: 'Catherine, *you* weren't speaking to them, God *was*', and he kissed my hand. The Reverend Mother kissed me and said: 'I don't think you need to stay any longer. It is going to take a long time to absorb what you said.'

Catherine had a big influence in the 1960s on many religious congregations and orders. It was during this period that she wrote the poem, 'What Is a Nun?'

A nun is a woman
Who believes in the Absolute,
And arises in search of it,
Laughing at all who
Speak of the impossibility of it.
For a woman who is a nun,
Knows that the impossible
Becomes the possible
In a matter of seconds,
At the bidding of her Beloved.

A nun is a woman who has become mad,
Totally, irrevocably mad!
For she has accepted
The standard of God's wisdom
Which is in truth folly to man.

A nun is a woman
Hanging on the other
Side of his cross
Knowing that it becomes
His marriage bed with her
The moment she asks
'To be lifted up' with him.

A nun is a woman
Of the water and the towel
Constantly kneeling before
Mankind to wash its
Tired feet.

A nun is a woman
In love with God — hence with all humanity
Always. . . constantly. . . totally. . .!

A nun is a prayer —
Everlastingly lifting her arms to God
For those who don't.

A nun is a woman
Who fasts
Knowing well how fast fast
Reaches
The heart of God.

A nun is a woman
Wrapped in the
Poverty of God
The mantle of
His surrender, his emptying!

A nun is a woman
Who exists
To show that God exists too.

It was during her interview with Pope Pius XII that he said to her, 'Madam, we need stable, dedicated lay people who will defend the Church, who will restore the Church, because the Church is about to suffer again.' She writes: 'This is the essence of our apostolate, this is why our apostolate exists. He foresaw what would be needed in the Church. Like Our Lady, we said yes. We stood for years under the cross of Christ. That's why we hold on to Mary. She knew what it was to stand there.'

1954 was a very important year at Madonna House, a landmark in its historical development. Bishop Coudert, the Apostolic Vicar of the Yukon, asked Catherine to open a Madonna House in Whitehorse. So, on 13 June 1954, three staff members went there. Fr Cullinane would join them later as chaplain. They were to serve the native population and the many families of workers and immigrants. They gave out food and clothing, visited the sick, rendered all kinds of services, exactly as Catherine had done in her Toronto and Harlem Friendship Houses.

A second mission house was opened in Edmonton, Alberta, in 1955. It was called Marian Centre. Native Indians and the unemployed could receive meals and find a listening ear.

On 17 May 1957, the tenth anniversary of Madonna House in Combermere, several staff members arrived in Winslow, Arizona, to serve the poor Mexican people, and the Hopi and Navaho Indians in the area. In 1960 another mission was opened on Carriacou, a small island in the West Indies. These were followed by missions in Peru, Pakistan, Honduras, Israel, Balmorea (Texas), Aquia (Virginia), Ellenburg, New York, Ottawa, Toronto, and other cities in both Canada and the United States. Before Catherine's death, houses would be opened in France and England.

Eventually, some of these houses would close, but the vocation and ideal of Catherine to go to the poor on behalf of Christ and his Church would acquire a universal missionary dimension.

During his interview the Pope spoke of the family, and how to find a way to share with them the liturgy, the gospel, and the essentials of Christian community life. This led to the establishment of Cana Colony.

In a clearing near Benet Lake in Combermere you can see seven or eight wooden cabins, one for each family. There is a central cook house and also a chapel, Our Lady of the Lake. This is a part of the Madonna House apostolate. For six or seven weeks during the summer families come and live together for a week, experiencing Christian community and learning something of Catherine's spirituality.

Catherine's influence was growing more and more in Canada and the States and in the rest of the world, especially through her books. In 1975 her book *Poustinia* came out and, by all standards, it's on its way to becoming a spiritual classic of our times. Another best seller has been *The Gospel Without Compromise*, which is a collection of her editorials over the years in Restoration. A glance at the list of her works in the Appendix (p. 116) will reveal that from 1975 to her death Catherine published fourteen books. There is still a great deal more to come out, especially her correspondence.

Catherine continued to lecture. In October 1977 she spoke at the Atlantic City Charismatic Conference to more than 42,000 people.

There are now about 150 laymen, laywomen, and priests who belong to Madonna House.

In 1981 Catherine made her last pilgrimage to Rome. Accompanied by Fr Briere, she attended Pope John Paul's private Mass in the morning and met him for the first and last time. She held a conference for journalists and she was asked many questions about her more than fifty years of apostolic service to the Church and humanity.

During these years she was given many awards and expressions of respect and esteem. She has received the Pro Pontifice et Ecclesia Medal, the Holy Cross Medal of John XXIII, the Poverello Medal from the college of Steubenville, Ohio, the St Teresa of Avila Medal from St Benedict's College in Minnesota. One of her most outstanding awards is the Order of Canada, the highest civilian award for outstanding contribution to one's country.

One of the awards most dear to her was the Pius X Award given to her by Joseph Neuman of the Martin de Porres Society for contributions in the area of racial justice. Joe Neuman was a little boy in Harlem and often went to Friendship House where he met Catherine. Also making the presentation was an elderly black friend from the Friendship House era, together with a young girl, the grand-daughter of a former member of the Harlem Friendship House staff. Thus three generations were represented. On receiving the award Catherine said, 'Through my poor self three generations of Harlem belong to God.'

In the archives of Madonna House can be found many documents about the foundation, evolution, and development of Madonna House, about Catherine's life, about her ever deeper penetration into her vocation — the mystical identification with God, her Beloved, with whom, she used to say, she fell in love.

Since 1981, because of her failing health, Catherine stayed in Combermere almost all the time. From time to time she would go to the hospital for medical check-ups, but for the most part she was in her poustinia on the banks of the Madawaska.

Her poustinia became a place of pilgrimage for hundreds of people each year, staff and guests. They would come to ask her advice and counsel, or her prayers. On 7 April 1984, her spiritual director (and the director of the priests), Father Callahan, died. For some months afterwards Catherine was quite ill, and her own death was expected. By turns, members of the community kept vigil at her bedside day and night.

In St Catherine's hemitage there was a profound atmosphere of love and peace. As the months wore on she gradually said farewell to her earthly life and her spiritual family. More and more, until her death, she dwelt in what was once called *molchanie*, the 'immense silence of God'.

3

STRANGE COMMUNITY

'You are welcome', says the girl, a staff worker of Madonna House, as she meets me at the bus in the lovely little town of Combermere, Ontario. It is nearly suppertime and here and there someone passes carrying a package or two from shopping at one of the small markets near the bus stop. This area, with its many lovely lakes flanked by the neat little summer homes and cabins of those who frequent it in summer especially, is used to the visitors and the people are friendly. They smile at me as they pass.

While the girl does a few errands which are part of what they call the evening 'bus run', I sit in the car and wait. My mind goes back to that evening in Galilee when I first met Catherine Doherty, Foundress of Madonna House, and received an invitation to visit her community.

I had met Archbishop Joseph Raya who, after resigning as Archbishop of the Melkite-Greek Catholic Diocese of Haifa, Akko, Nazareth and all of Galilee, had arrived in Haifa. On this particular evening, I was sitting with Suzy, Mary Kay, Mary and Theresa, all members of Madonna House, who were working with the Bishop here in Haifa. It was a beautiful evening and we were enjoying a nice, sea breeze on the roof terrace.

At the harbour facing us, a number of boat lights were dancing on the Mediterranean Sea. Far away on the horizon we could discern the silhouette of the Hills of Galilee which separate Israel from Lebanon. Suddenly, someone was ringing the door bell.

It was Catherine de Hueck Doherty. The girls and the Bishop, who were all wearing the silver cross with the Pax Caritas inscription around their necks, rose to welcome their foundress. They introduced me to her. Catherine regarded me intently and then said: 'You are a priest. In you I greet Christ.' She kissed my hand and expressed her wish that I remain and share the evening.

She was a large, blonde lady with a round face and soft clear eyes. She wore a long, coloured dress and gave out a scent of oriental perfume. The particular accent with which she spoke betrayed the Russian origin. Frequently she would accentuate what she said with sweeping movements.

We talked about evangelisation and mission. 'Mission', she said suddenly, 'is the willingness to be used by others. It is availability without limits.' When I was about to leave, she said, 'Come and see Combermere. Come and pray with us and reflect with us upon how we can love God and the poor more ardently.' So here I was on this autumn evening waiting in this car to be taken to this place called Madonna House, and meet again this wonderful woman and her co-workers. I was excited at the prospect.

The girl returns and we drive off the main highway onto a wooded road. After about an eighth of a mile we turn into a parking lot surrounded by large, white buildings. Two of these are joined and are clearly the main house. As we enter the basement where we leave our wraps, I see over the door a motto which sums up the hospitality of Madonna House. In colourful letters it reads: 'There are no strangers here — only friends we haven't met.' We leave our wraps and ascend the stairs leading into the main dining-room which is also the library and common room.

It is a large, pleasant room, but very simple. The floor is just rough board, unpainted. The wood panelling on the walls is lined with shelves on which there are books of many kinds. The furniture is very simple; the room is filled with heavy wooden tables at each of which six people are seated on benches having supper. Upon entering, one hears a flow of happy, lively conversation punctuated with lots of laughter. Here and there young women pass to and fro between the kitchen and dining-room carrying dishes of hot food or large, enamelled pots of tea. (I leaned later that on Sundays the men give their sisters a rest and they do the serving.) The atmosphere is relaxed and peaceful.

Bishop Raya, my friend from Israel, comes to welcome me and then I see Catherine hastening to greet me. She is wearing a long, yellow dress with green flowers. 'Welcome, Father! Welcome home!' she says. 'We are so glad to see you!' I get a round of applause from those present, all of whom have risen. Later I learn that they do this whenever a priest enters. Catherine explains: 'We do not stand up for you, Father. We rise because of the Christ in you.'

I was ushered to a place at the head of the rough wooden table with Bishop Raya. 'Priests are always given a place of honour.'

Catherine explains, 'You see we have a great respect and love for priests. We recognise Jesus in the priest. That too, is the reason why we never call you by your first names, but always address you as "Father".' I greatly enjoyed the simple meal which I learnt came largely from the farm miles away. Here, at this farm, most of the food is grown and processed.

Before I leave the dining-room, I look around a bit. Here on the walls are various pictures of Catherine and people who have played an important part in her life and in that of the apostolate of which she is foundress. There are many nice plants on the window sills which show a love of beauty even in the simplicity. One area displays the many books which have been written here and which are for sale. Beneath a special lighting arrangement is a large icon done by the staff iconographer. I note various printed sayings here and there on the wall. Often I am told these are things Catherine says frequently. My mind is arrested by one which reads: 'I am Third.' A staff worker explains: 'This means that God must always come first in my life, my neighbour second, and myself, last.'

The staff worker goes on to explain: 'We are a Christian community — a family of men and women, as you see, and a number of our men are priests. We are in love with God here and everything begins and ends with him.' One notices how often the conversation turns to God and the things of God. This occurs very spontaneously and naturally for he is their whole life — their reason for being here.

After the evening meal, there are chores to be done. The women go to the kitchen to wash the dishes. There is a happy, relaxed atmosphere despite a large kitchen crowded with women putting away food, washing and drying the dishes, dismantling trays which have come from the sick, taking out the garbage to the compost heap. (Nothing is wasted here. Everything that can be is recycled.) Some sweep and wash the floor. Others are setting the tables in the dining room. Often they break into song together and what could be a chore becomes a pleasant, happy event — a fostering of togetherness and co-operation. The men repair to the basement where they peel and cut up tomorrow's vegetables around a large table. A flow of pleasant conversation accompanies this. All the men help. One sees a priest who was at the evening liturgy peeling onions beside a young visitor from the city, who is learning how to deal with a turnip. A woman staff worker is overseeing the whole operation. A great feeling of belonging is fostered as visitors are drawn immediately into family activities. These visitors who 'are but friends we haven't met' are right away made to feel responsible for, and a part of the family. There is a peace and serenity as all work together on these various projects which are sometimes called 'bees'.

Every evening around 5.00 p.m. the priest members of Madonna House, and any priests who are visiting, concelebrate the liturgy in the beautiful Byzantine chapel in the woods near Madonna House. Before the Mass, the main celebrant bows his head and asks his fellow priests to bless him. (I note in the sacristy another saying: 'My brother is my life'.) At this liturgy, one sees young people from many countries: from Latin America, Asia, Europe, Africa, Japan. There are a number of visiting priests like myself and a few sisters too. All come in search of a deeper union with God through this simple, Gospel way of life. They sense the peace and serenity here which renews them and sends them back to their own spiritual roots.

On Sundays the liturgy is celebrated with greater splendour. The Sunday after my arrival there are twenty priests concelebrating. Bishop Raya is the main celebrant of the beautiful Byzantine liturgy which is carried out in all its splendour. I see that the staff, especially the schola, are well trained in celebrating this liturgy. Here East and West meet in a symphony of worship. The wooden chapel is filled with beautiful Slavic and Greek tones. A male staff member of the schola who, a few moments before was wearing jeans and a plaid shirt, and is now dressed in a black skofa and jibbe, steps before the iconostasis and expertly proclaims a Prokeimenon. After the liturgical celebration, a number of men and women walk to the front and lovingly venerate the icons. Some bow low, touching the floor, and then make the Sign of the Cross.

During the final hymn, Catherine breaks out into a dance before the icons. She is joined by a group of staff workers and the celebration ends in an alleluia — an apotheosis of singing and dancing worship. It is beautiful to see this lovely, free expression of love of God and his liturgy. During his homily, the Bishop had mentioned that Christianity spells joy and liberation because God's love and beauty live in all people. 'Because', he had explained, 'Christ is risen and that is JOY!' He had added, 'Let's be happy and let our joy be known to all people.' He had spoken of the face of God smiling at us through the icons and through the faces of all people.

This evening, among the people joining in the liturgy are Dr Joseph McKenna, a physician and friend of Madonna House from Toronto, who periodically visits and cares for the sick. He has a great love for and interest in Madonna House. Also present is Bishop Omer Delaquis from Gravelbourg, Saskatchewan, the man who a few years later was to become an associate priest of Madonna House. The joy and fraternal spirit emanating from all here — both guests and staff — can hardly be expressed in words. Around the Table of the Lord, they are one big, happy family, and it is expressed in the joy on their faces as they dance with Catherine or just appreciate the dance from where they stand.

Later I have the opportunity to meet and talk with many of these young and old visitors whom I had had the opportunity to observe at the liturgy and in the dining room. I found that the lay people, young and old, as well as the priests, have discovered here a deep meaning in life and death; have witnessed something special in the lives of these people at Combermere; have felt that they have witnessed a special love of God incarnated daily in little things; have witnessed a special joy and a special meaning in humble tasks. It has helped them to deepen their own spiritual life and to witness to a deeper call to greater generosity and loyalty in their own callings. Some could express it better than others, but it was easy to detect a depth of fulfilment in all who came and participated in this way of life. Many had felt the deep witness of love that traverses nationality, age and walk of life. Some said they were aware of a personal dignity they had not felt before. Each person coming here is seen as Christ coming — as a beloved child of the Father — and this dignity as a child of God surpasses rank or age. There was something beautiful to see at the end of a communal penance celebration when Bishop Raya went to kneel for forgiveness at the feet of Father David, the youngest priest present.

I asked Father Gene Cullinane, who has been a member of Madonna House for thirty years, how he felt about the influence of the community on others. He said: 'Here God is present in ·a special way. This may sound triumphalistic or conceited, but it was precisely this same spirit expressed by the others that knocked me off my horse when I arrived here after many years of involvement as a priest in a religious community. God simply does unusual things here.'

Father Gene told me too, how people initially questioned the fact that both men and women live and work together in this community. This sort of thing was quite unheard of when Madonna House was first founded and it was rather suspect. He said they asked jokingly what happened to all the babies born here. He told them: 'You will find out that when people, because of their love of God and because of their radical faith in the Gospel, really love each other because it is their special calling, there cannot be any serious problem.'

Fr John Callahan said: 'When we find out that there is a particular love relationship beginning between two people, we speak out from the community: "Look here, this is not where your vocation lies." In a community where prayer, the Gospel and the Church are the backbone of our lives and of our being together, one learns to be honest with God, with oneself, with each other and with those in charge. Maybe in this intuitive approach to life and the everyday reality of our community here, we are simpler, more honest and more balanced than in some exclusively male or female religious communities."

Those who stay at Madonna House will very soon find out what it means for the staff members and the visitors to live a life of true, radical, evangelical poverty. With the exception of Vianney House (the house for the priests at Carmel Hill), where there are single rooms for the priests and visiting clergy, everybody sleeps in common dorms. Dorms for the women are on the same premises as Madonna House proper; those for the men are a few miles away. In each dorm there is a small linen cupboard, a bathroom (except for the dorm-cabins where outside toilets are used and water is carried in and out for washing), and a place to hang clothes. Privacy is one of the luxuries the poor do not have, and is one of those luxuries the staff worker surrenders in this life of poverty. So is space. Each staff worker has a small stand or a covered orange crate beside his or her bed and some space in a small cupboard. One quickly learns dispossession.

When staff workers need a garment of some sort, they go to get it in the common clothing room of which there is one for the men and one for the women staff. Everyone wears second-hand clothing. But they are nicely dressed because these donations are varied and often quite nice. On Sundays the men will often wear their best second-hand suit and the women a long skirt and colourful blouse or another 'special' outfit. 'It is the day of the Lord', they say, 'and we try to look our best'. These are the men and women you will meet next day in their jeans or rough working clothes at St Benedict's Farm or around Madonna House. One cannot tend pigs and chickens, shovel manure, do cleaning or garden work in good clothing. Besides, it is second-hand and needs special care to last. The women become experts in patchng, darning and otherwise making clothes go a long way.

Madonna House has always taught a real reverence for manual work — for doing the 'little things well'! They even have a song about it. Catherine has written a book, *People of the Towel and Water*, which grew from outlines she had previously written for the various work departments of Madonna House. She realised that many come with a wrong impression of what is important in life. Many feel that they derive their importance in life by what they *do*. With a hundred or more people at Madonna House at any given time, there are a great deal of tasks many would call menial — a word shunned at Madonna House. No work is menial if it is done with love to serve Christ in our brother. 'Christ', Catherine always explains, 'took a basin and towel and went around serving — washing his disciples' feet. . . a task usually reserved for servants in an Eastern household. We too, must serve in all so-called ways with great love.

Young people who wish to become members of Madonna House, or even to visit for a while, learn to work in the many departments and to do their work well, be it farming, gardening, washing, ironing, cleaning, washing dishes, sewing or sorting clothes for the poor. They go to the laundry, the workshop, the gardens, etc. The priests, as well as the other men, work. Some do carpentry, help with the sorting, do editing, give retreats, write books and give spiritual direction. They learn what cooking means and they are no strangers to a broom and a mop. They too believe in what Catherine was always saying: 'Love serves'. The life of Madonna House is not possble without asceticism and abstinence. This is seen in this sample of the order and regularity at Madonna House (and the necessity for the right motivation) as set out in the daily schedule:

7.00	. . . . Rising
8.00	. . . . Morning prayer of Lauds
8.30	. . . . Breakfast
9.00	. . . . Work assignments
12.00	. . . . Dinner — followed by spiritual reading

1.10	.... Back to work
3.30	.... Afternoon tea break
5.15	.... Mass
6.00	.... Supper
8.00	.... Various courses on many nights such as: liturgy and scripture, Fathers of the Church, Christian ethics, Church history, or schola practice for some
9.00	.... Evening tea and recreation
10.00	.... Singing of Salve Regina and departure for the various domitories
11.15	.... Lights out

One day I am driven six miles up the road to St Benedict's, the Madonna House farm. It is situated on a hill overlooking a valley which, in the autumn, is absolutely resplendent with reds, oranges and yellows. The maples in this area really dress up to meet Jack Frost! Beautiful brown and white Ayrshire cattle graze lazily behind the massive barns. Large, black Percheron horses in the pasture raise their heads to see who or what is arriving. A medium-grown black filly trots away to join her mother in the field beyond. Bessie, the Great Pyrenees dog who is being trained to guard the sheep, comes to meet us, wagging her tail and barking quite unconvincingly. A young woman carrying a large tray of bread comes out of the house and places it in an outdoor oven to bake. The air here is cool and sweet, and an atmosphere of wholesomeness and peace prevails. I am told that everyone likes to be sent up to the farm to work.

On the hilltop behind the barns is a cross set into a pile of stones. It is a beautiful symbol of the One to whom this farm and its work is dedicated. Joseph Hogan, one of their farmers, explains its significance: 'For me it is a symbol of the earth redeemed. Every morning you see the sun rise behind the cross as a symbol of the Resurrection of Christ. It is not only the seed in the soil that means growth. The secret of the farm is the dedication of the men and women. We all made the promises of poverty, chastity and obedience for life, and some of us will remain on this farm for the rest of our lives. The first priority of our farm is prayer. Without contact with God, our life would be sad and meaningless. Every day the farmers pray Lauds and Vespers and attend Mass in the chapel in the loft of the small farmhouse at 11.30 a.m.

'The second priority is friendship. Everyone who desires to stay at our farm is welcomed with true love. Our way of life is based on the Gospel and on the philosophy of Catherine Doherty. We try to include the whole world and our lives testify to an apostolic simplicity. The profit of our work is donated to the poor. We ourselves live on what others give us. Apostolic farming, that is what Catherine calls the farm work. While seven men with promises for life live a life of prayer, work and mutual love here, every year many others — both men and women — come here for some time (the women come in the daytime only to cook and process food), to share this life so as to become, in Madonna House, farmers of God.'

After Mass the farmers share their frugal meal with the guests in the long, narrow kitchen of the farmhouse. After dinner, the priest who has offered Mass with them reads a passage from the Gospel or from some spiritual book, followed by reflection and discussion. After this, the farmers resume their exceptionally hard work.

I learn that the formation of a staff worker at Madonna House takes eight or nine years before they take final promises in the community. There are two years of applicancy before which most have spent some time here as a working guest. During this time there is a lot of study and training in various departments. During this time too, applicants have a good opportunity to see how well they fit into this way of life and the community has a good chance to observe them. If, after this time, both applicant and community feel it is God's will for them to continue (for that is the greatest criterion of all), then the applicant takes promises of poverty, chastity and obedience for a year and becomes a staff worker. After the year, if the applicant is to continue, promises are made for a two-year period. This is renewed three times for a two-year period and after this time the staff worker makes promises for life. During these two-year periods (and sometimes during the one-year period), the staff worker goes for a while to a field house to obtain experience working with a smaller group in a possibly more demanding situation.

Since 1947 when Madonna House was founded, Catherine has been the guiding force and inspiration for this little community, assisted by some of the older staff who take on a lot of responsibility and, of course, the priests, who are ever ready to give spiritual help as the spiritual directors of the staff and applicants, and who often work side by side with them as well.

There are twenty-one field houses: eleven in Canada (besides Madonna House itself), seven in the United States, one in France, one in England and one in Barbados, West Indies. Sometimes a staff worker is sent out alone to engage in some sort of apostolic activity, but this is rare. Each year sees bishops requesting a foundation in various parts of the world, and a good number of candidates applying to live this way of life.

Upon being asked how they decide which places to go to when many are asking for Madonna Houses, the staff will say that the Holy Spirit has to decide that. No request is accepted without much prayer and discernment on the part of the community, for Madonna House is Our Lady's House and it is her spouse, the Holy Spirit, who is its chief guiding force in all decisions regarding it.

4

SPIRITUALITY

During the early years of her apostolate, Catherine met with misunderstanding and even hostility from Canadians and Americans who had trouble accepting her radical vision of God and of the incarnation of the Gospel. She had a very direct and sometimes even brutal way of expressing herself, which did not help matters. North American society saw human beings and human life in a rationalistic way, and because she came from a culture that thought and spoke of God in a warm, human fashion, her adaptation and integration were rendered all the more difficult.

For Westerners, action for God is much more important than it is in the East, where the emphasis, first and foremost, is on 'being' before God. Feeling the tension between these two visions, Catherine was driven to protect, like a treasure in her heart, this Russian heritage in which the theology, spirituality and liturgy of the Byzantine Church had such an important place. On the other hand, she strove, in her contacts and apostolic outreach, to adapt her techniques and methods to the milieu in which she was now living.

Subsequent to the foundation of Madonna House, and after she had become more adapted to and even appreciated in Canada and the United States, Catherine began to write and speak more openly of the Russian heritage which so obviously influenced the daily life and spirituality of Madonna House.

Interior life and contemplation
The attention given to the interior life is apparent in the daily schedule of the community. For the members of Madonna House, living in God is every bit as natural as breathing. If one is to do God's work, living in him, with him and for him is a necessary prerequisite. Charity and action proceed from the spiritual life.

Catherine gives an important place in her spirituality to contemplation. 'Contemplation is an irresistible need, based on the search for the Kingdom of God in our own hearts. When the noise inside us and outside us becomes unbearable, we must not hesitate to divest ourselves of everything. It is then that we discover the heart of our life: the uninterrupted contemplation of God.'

In contemplation, the Trinitarian dimension of faith is strongly accentuated. 'Madonna House's main aim is to form a community of love. The word community is as old as the universe and older, for it is a word that belongs to eternity. The eternal community is the Trinity. In order to form a community, you must make contact with the Trinity first. . . no community can be established among people if it decides it does not need Jesus, or that it can make itself God. When we fall in love with God, with the Trinity, we become part of that eternal and primary Community of Love.'

Eucharist and prayer

Contemplation means that much time has to be given to prayer. Catherine was overwhelmed when priests came to join the apostolate, since theirs was the function of presiding over the liturgy.

Each day of the week, a community Mass is celebrated by the Madonna House priests in what is called the island chapel, surrounded by tall pine trees. On Sundays, the Latin Mass alternates with the Divine Liturgy sung in the Byzantine Rite.

During each daily celebration, the most important elements of this lay apostolate are recalled and professed in the presence of the Eucharistic Christ, i.e. the total gift of one's life to the Trinitarian God, the sharing of one's possessions with the poor, and the evangelical community life in the spirit of love to which the members of Madonna House are called. 'If any group of people need the Mass, we apostles of the marketplace do. . . we could not exist without it, nor persevere in our new, strange, and seemingly radical vocation of organised Christian action. We could not even begin to try to practise the counsels of perfection, stability and dedication, unless we daily came to the Food of the poor man. Only in him, with him and through him could we achieve our goal. . . All things can be endured and all things become possible between two Masses: the Mass of yesterday and the Mass of tomorrow. I need to be able to sustain one day of my life. I need him daily because I am a sinner and weak. When we have a Mass in the evening, I am eager all day for it — it is so much a part of me. I receive so much from him, sharing with the whole world the faith and the unity that are there. To live without the Eucharist would be like asking me to live without a heart.'

The collective and community prayer at Madonna House is also the expression and sign of faith in the need to listen to God and to speak to him, in order to live for God consciously, day after day.

'How can any Christian community, be it one of religious, lay people, married people or celibates, live this life of a pilgrim, this life of listening to the heart of man and to the Spirit, if it does not pray?'

'What is impossible to man becomes possible to God. To persevere, one must pray without ceasing. We make the Eucharist the heart of our life, and thus we live in union with God in prayer. Otherwise, we will lose contact with human beings. Such is the message addressed by Catherine to her followers.

During liturgical prayer, songs are sung by men and women *a capella*, often in polyphony, and the music is influenced by the Slavic and Greek tones of the Byzantine liturgy. A remarkable sense of peace and of the sacred emanates from these moments of prayer. Many young people participate in the community prayer and it is moving to watch them pray and sing, not ony because the liturgy at Madonna House is particularly well carried out, but because there is, in these young people, an authentic and strong will and desire to pray. One sees men and women in prayer during the day and sometimes late at night, in the island chapel, in the oratory above the main dining room and in the attic chapel at the farm. Kneeling or seated, they are lost in contemplation of the God Who is Trinity.

In the chapel of Vianney House, one sees priests spending innumerable hours of night-time adoration, or beginning the day very early in the morning with several hours of prayer.

One of the most common forms of prayer in Madonna House is the famous Jesus Prayer. The invocation, 'Lord Jesus Christ, Son of the Living God, have mercy on me a sinner' is often recommended as a simple form of constant, interior prayer. Theological reflections centred around the Jesus Prayer may be suggested as material for personal meditation.

It is in this perspective that the short invocations and expressions so often heard around Madonna House must be understood. Spontaneous phrases such as 'God bless', 'Thank God', 'Praise the Lord', 'Alleluia', are modes of expression natural to those who live by prayer and contemplation. To some extent, they witness to the influence of the Charismatic Renewal, which touched so many North Americans in the 1960s and 1970s.

Poustinia

One day in 1961, as Catherine was walking through some of the Madonna House property, she was struck by the style of an old, abandoned farmhouse nearby. Suddenly the idea came to her to transform this little building into a hermitage. She went in. It was a very simple wooden house, comprising one small room and one large room on the ground floor, and three small rooms on the second floor. She stayed there for hours, seated on the threshold of the house, and thinking of the little Russian dwellings, astonishingly similar to this, which served as poustinias.

Returning to the main house, she spoke with members of the staff about these Russian poustinias, and her dream of transplanting this eremitical practice to Madonna House and North America. In September 1962 she asked the local directors to begin setting up or, if need be, building poustinias.

Ideally, the poustinia consists of one room. In Combermere, it is usually a log cabin containing a wood stove and a kerosene lamp. There are a table and chairs, a Bible, something to write with, a hard bed on which to rest or sleep. Hanging on the wall is a large cross, three feet by six feet or thereabouts, without a corpus. This symbolises the death through which each person must pass in order to resurrect with Christ. In the eastern corner of the room is an icon of Our Lady; in another corner is a pitcher and basin in which to wash. On a shelf there are a cup, tea, a bread-board and a knife, a plate or two.

One normally goes to the poustinia for twenty-four hours, with the permission of a spiritual director. One brings a loaf of bread and a thermos of hot water or milk, to provide a little nourishment. In silence, solitude and fasting, the poustinik meets God person-to-person, and hears his voice speaking in their own heart or through the Scriptures. On their return from the poustinia, poustinikki often bring to the community a word which God has given them.

At Madonna House, Combermere, poustinias are built with logs, the available building material. In the field houses, rooms are reserved wherever possible for use as poustinias. At present, there are approximately twenty poustinias in use at Combermere. Three priest members of the community and one woman live permanently in poustinias on the island where Catherine also lives. Three days a week (and for some a longer time), they remain alone in their poustinia, spending the rest of the time with the community. Most members of the staff spend a day, a week, or one day a month in poustinia. Thus, the poustinia experience has become an important aspect of Madonna House life.

When Catherine first began speaking about the poustinia in 1962, she saw it as the answer to many problems threatening the world and the Church. She wrote:

> I have no other answer than my poustinia, which for me means prayer, penance, mortification, solitude and silence. All these offered in a spirit of love, atonement, reparation to God according to the spirit of the old prophets: intercession before God for our fellow man, for our brothers in Christ, whom I and all of us in Madonna House love so passionately in him, for they are him: The poustinia is a place to which the lay people must go in order to gather courage to speak words of truth, remembering that truth is God, and that he proclaims the Word of God. The poustinia will cleanse him, and prepare him to do so, like the coal that the angel placed on the lips and tongue of the prophet.

The poustinia experience has become known especially through the publication of Catherine's Book *Poustinia: Christian Spirituality of the East for Western Man*, (Ave Maria Press, Notre Dame, Indiana, 1975). Within a short time, 10,000 copies had been sold. Several years later, the book had been translated into all the important languages of the world. It was a bestseller that seemed to respond to a deep need: the need for silence and to meet God.

Nevertheless, it is important to realise that the experience of the poustinia is not tied to a particular place. In our Western world, which is a highly structured, technological and industrial society, it is not always possible to find a log cabin surrounded by forest, or even a calm, deserted spot in which this desert experience can take place. That is why Catherine has spoken so repeatedly of the 'poustinia of the heart', always coming back to the Little Mandate. Even in the busy traffic and noise of a large city, amid the worries and activity of daily life, the poustinia can be lived in the depths of one's heart.

'Go into the marketplace and stay with me. . .' Thanks to the poustinia, the richness received in the heart is brought to the world, into the heart of the world.

> . . .Slowly, imperceptibly, the world around them will change. For the silence within will become part of God's loving, mighty, creative, fecund silence, and his voice will be heard through them, and his face will be seen in theirs. . . and the light of it will become a light to their neighbour's feet. Thus silence will bring peace to all. And the prayer of silence will be heard in our land, far and wide.

Whatever form or location the poustinia takes, 'those who enter a poustinia must remember always the vertical descent of Christ from the Father, his horizontal life as a man, and his vertical ascent to the Father after his resurrection.'

For the members of Madonna House, the poustinia is the link between the active and the contemplative life. In Catherine's perspective, all Christians by virtue of their baptism, are both contemplative and active. 'Perhaps, God willing, this simple, humble life of prayer and service and of unity between the two immense streams of Christianity will bring forth deeper unity of same in the Church. Who can tell?' she wrote in one of her *Letters from the Poustinia*, (Combermere, 10 August 1970, p. 11).

The life of Nazareth
'The spirit of Madonna House is the spirit of Nazareth — of a family — of the family of Nazareth which was a community of perfect charity and love.' 'If people ask you, "What is the apostolate of Madonna House?" you answer simply, "It is an apostolate of love, for where love is, God is," and the rest will follow. That's all there is to it.'

In the *Little Mandate*, Catherine wrote, 'Be little. . . be always little. . . be simple, poor, childlike. Do little things exceedingly well for love of me.' And in a letter addressed to members of the community, she wrote, 'Nazareth is our model, our spiritual home, a community of love in a self-forgetfulness and the total surrender of one's self to the will of God. To be involved in simple daily life, monotonous, routine, but filled with small tasks carried out with a great love for God and neighbour. . . it seems that

God needs to reveal himself in the most ordinary things of life.'

This spirituality has been described in a very poignant way in *People of the Towel and the Water*, (Dimension Books, New York, 1978). One can easily take this book as a manual for any contemplative community where manual work is present, and the need to relate to God himself the little things in life. . . Members of Madonna House and the many friends of the community consider it to be one of the most important writings Catherine has given them.

Anyone who stays at Madonna House is struck by the attention, respect and love with which dishes are washed, the earth cultivated, hospitality given, and so many other ordinary activities, necessary to the organisation and life of such a large group of people living together in this type of community, carried on.

In Madonna House, each person feels involved in the family life of Nazareth, where the mystique of the cross and poverty both play an important role.

Mystique of the cross and life of poverty

The *Little Mandate* also includes the following words: 'Take up your cross and follow me'. In meditations and in conversation, Catherine often used the image of the Christian who becomes cruciform, touching God with one hand and man with the other.

To die to self and consciously to accept physical and spiritual sacrifices is a necessary condition for sanctification. Catherine emphasised the centrality of the cross, placing a large, naked cross in each poustinia.

Throughout her whole life, Catherine was moved by the ideal of poverty expressed by the Poverello. 'The Lord took me by the hand', she wrote 'and led me step by step, anticipating the needs of the Church. The first need was that of poverty. I knew that whatever we did as a little group, we must be beggars, because so many people in the Church were rich. I did not know, at that time, of the wealth of the Orders, but I surmised it. I sensed that St Francis had the real answer before Brother Elias weakened his work by building all those monasteries. I felt that our apostolate too, had to be Franciscan, but in a very modern Francican way, allowing for great freedom and with practically no structures.

'In 1930, this was not the thing to do! It was rebellion. Only Archbishop Neil McNeil understood what I had in mind, and he covered me with the mantle of his office so that I was able to survive. Eventually I was forced out of Toronto by public pressure. The words of Father Carr at that time still ring in my ears: "They hate you because you are doing what they should be doing".'

The next need within the Church was for some people to identify with the poor. A few people have the specific vocation to identify with the poor by living near them, among them, sharing their life. In Toronto and New York, Catherine became one of them. 'We must become poor', she said, 'because being poor with the poor means to become like Christ'. 'Because I was lecturing and constantly being questioned by everyone, I recognised the need to *live by the Gospel*. The only answers I gave people were from the Gospel, from the Scriptures. I realised then that what the Church, the people of God needed was the strong food of the Holy Scriptures. All those intellectual sermons, so prominent in those days, were getting the Church nowhere. . . So I started teaching the liturgy and the Scriptures, because these were crying needs of the people of God.

'. . .But the pain was growing. I began to realise that anyone who accepts the Gospel without compromise will not only become a wound, but a wound into which many people will constantly pour salt.'

During the years spent in the slums, Catherine had been able to recognise heroic witnesses in that jungle of misery, unemployment, hunger and unimaginable poverty. She insisted that the Church had need of martyrs. 'Not big, spectacular martyrs but little martyrs, little beggars, poor people to live with the poor. The Church needed people to teach the gospel and the liturgy in order not to compromise the gospel.'[1]

In her love for the little ones — the homeless, the prisoners, the hungry, the poor lost in the great cities, she nevertheless always retained a concern for the spiritually poor. She wanted to unite herself with them also. This became clear during the sixties: the years of the Vatican Council, which brought uncertainty to so many religious communities, among so many Christians and young people.

In our own times, when the Church and efforts towards evangelisation are influenced by materialism, secularisation, and the decline of spiritual life, Madonna House, in accordance with

---

[1] *Fragments of My Life*, pp. 201-202.

Catherine's spirit of poverty, desires to be a home for all who are hungry for God and who no longer know where to turn in their despair, their bitterness and disappointment, their unhappiness. It wishes to be a place where people can learn to fill their lives with love for God and for all men. Those who are poor in this sense have a special place in the spirituality of Madonna House.

Friday is a fast day at Madonna House. Usually it is only on Sundays that there is meat on the table. Butter too is reserved for Sundays and feast days. We have already talked about second-hand clothing, dormitory living, and the giving away of all extra monies as signs of a life of radical poverty. Young people who wish to become members of Madonna House, who have taken part in this Western consumer society, understand well what they will have to give up, but their choice is free and deliberate. Anyone who wishes to live such a vocation must have a great love for God, for the poor, and for the Church.

Love for the Church

'I have always loved the Church — for anyone who is in love with God, the Church is a reality of faith. It is hard to explain that intellectually. One must put one's hand on one's heart, close one's eyes and adore a reality that can be apprehended only through faith.'

The relationship between the Church, people of God and Mystical Body of Christ, has always attracted her. In her work, *Dear Father* (Alba House, New York, 1978), her love for the Church and for priests is expressed very movingly.

'From the very beginning of my apostolate, when I sold everything I owned, God has given me a great love for the Church and for her priests. This Church cannot die. Call me naive or crazy, for I am, but the Church is precious to me, and I will continue to love her. Furthermore, I see clearly that Christ lives in her in a visible way.'

Each time an important decision is to be taken in Madonna House, the advice and authorisation of the local bishop are sought. The person of the Pope, of bishops and of priests, send us back explicitly to Jesus who, thanks to them, lives among us.

Marian devotion

Beginning in Combermere, where it took on its particular form, Catherine called her apostolic movement Madonna House: the House of Mary.

*Along Route 517, at the entrance to **Madonna House**.*

Archbishop Joseph Raya,
Madonna House priest.

The central house of Madonna House in Combermere.

Staff members and guests in the refectory.

Poustinia-followers — a life for God, the Beloved.

Evening eucharist.

Healing service.

Poustinia-houses close to Carmel Hill.

The Vianney-house for priests on Carmel Hill.

Lunch at the farm.

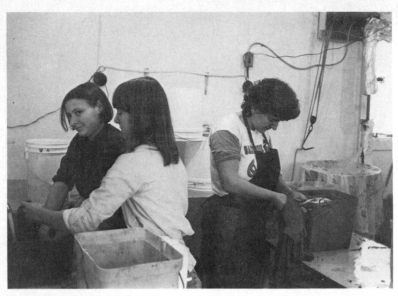

Manual work at the farm.

Catherine Doherty and Father Omer Tanghe, in Paris, just before her press-conference in St. Leu-St. Gilles on March 22, 1981.

Grave of Catherine de Hueck Doherty — Combermere graveyard.

Cleaning the dishes and manual work after the meals.

Stake with names of the fieldhouses.

Our Lady of Combermere —
bronze statue.

Graveyard of staff members of Madonna House at the local cemetery of Combermere.

The wooden chapel.

Catherine herself, as well as her second husband, Eddie Doherty, had a great devotion to Mary, the Theotokos, the Mother of God. When Fr John Callahan came to stay permanently at Madonna House in 1952, and became Catherine's spiritual director, he brought his own deep, personal devotion to Our Lady, in which the act of total consecration to Jesus through Mary of St Louis Marie Grignion de Montfort had an important consecration to Our Lady. Each evening the day ends with the singing of the Salve Mater, addressed to the Protectors of the Madonna House family of Combermere and of its twenty-one mission houses.

Lay community

It is important not to forget that Madonna House is a community centred on the lay apostolate. The members of Madonna House are consecrated to the Church of life through the three evangelical vows, but with the exception of the priests, they remain lay persons. They wear no special garb, and are distinguished only by a metal cross bearing the words Pax Caritas, which each member receives after making their first promises. Staff workers of Madonna House may live a contemplative life, but they are not religious in the canonical sense. They wish to live out, as lay people, in a particular fashion, their vocation to the lay apostolate. 'Ours is the age of the laity', they say, 'but we wish to live this lay state in a specific way, in the context of this family of men and women, inspired by the Gospel. This is why we want to work and witness in the tradition of Catholic Action, of the Legion of Mary, of the Charismatic Renewal, of the Young Catholic Workers, with an accent on the poor, the lonely, the victims of our society, taking as our examples the great lay saints and witnesses: Frank Duff, Caryll Houselander, Chesterton, Thomas More, Matt Talbot, Dorothy Day, and Catherine Doherty herself.'

This lay characteristic is, in fact, regularly emphasised by staff workers of Madonna House. Al Osterberger, currently director of the farm, is a former US Air Force officer. He served during the Korean War and later held an important position in an electronics firm in the United States. He found his way to Madonna House after having read in *The Seven-Storey Mountain*, Thomas Merton's autobiography, the story of the author's encounter with Catherine Doherty. Al Osterberger was also struck by the announcement in a magazine during the fifties of a summer school session at Combermere for the lay apostolate. There he met Catherine, who talked to him of the possibilities open to him — he was looking for God and for his own vocation — as a layman, in a life of work and prayer in the context of Madonna House. Al became a member. To a journalist who was questioning hm about his new identity he said: 'Ours is an apostolate of lay people and is very close to the first Christian communities, who also wanted to remain lay people. There are many things which are possible for us to do for Jesus and for the poor precisely because we are not religious — that is, bound to a religious rule. Still, we are bound to God and to the Church, as lay people, by our promises of chastity, poverty and obedience.'

Associate members

Bishop Joseph Raya was Greek Catholic Archbishop of Haifa, Akko and all of Galilee in Israel from 1968-74. He now lives at Madonna House apart from retreat work and teaching at the John XXIII Institute for Eastern Studies at Fordham University in New York. Bishop Raya first visited Madonna House during the fifties when he was a parish priest in Alabama. When he saw the Madonna House cross, he asked one of the Madonna House priests to give him one of these. He insisted he wanted to wear this cross with Pax Caritas on it, even though he was not a member of Madonna House.

Catherine and Father Callahan thought it over and prayed about it. After much prayer, they decided that the request of this priest was an invitation from God to establish a religious fraternity for secular priests, and later also for permanent deacons who would live the spirituality of Madonna House in their respective dioceses, in the context of their own ministries. Thus there was a historic moment when Bishop Raya received his cross and became an associate member. This was the hand of God writing another chapter in the saga of Madonna House. Catherine, who so loved priests, was to have many priest-sons in the many associates who would receive this cross and participate in her way of life.

The associate members, most of whom live in Canada and the United States, also have priest brothers in Africa, in the West Indies, in Europe, and in Asia. They become members after a trial period of one year, after which they too make their promises which they can renew after a year. After three years, they are allowed to make final promises. They also wear the cross engraved with 'Pax Caritas'. In the context of their lives, as bishop, priest or deacon, they help to propagate and incarnate the message of Catherine Doherty and of Madonna House. They are part of what Catherine often calls 'The Training Centre for the Lay Apostolate'. Members of Madonna House are always proud to boast of a priest in their class. 'We are family', Catherine says. 'We are all children of Our Lady of Combermere living in a house that belongs to her. Our spiritual home is Nazareth; the Holy Family is our model.'

These associate members cannot be present here to have classes with the other members, but they are trained in the Madonna House spirit by receiving Madonna House literature from time to time. They are kept in close touch with all that goes on here. Each autumn there is a three-day retreat for the associate priests when they come for talks, discussions, for various contacts with the family, and for an evening when all staff members, priestly and otherwise, get together for just a general good sharing and fun. In spirit, these priests feel close to the Madonna House family to which they belong by a special arrangement, and they frequently write newsletters telling of their work and asking for prayers. Several remarked to me what a strength it is to have the loving support of this family, and to know that they can turn to it for spiritual 'ammunition'.

Through Bishop Raya, the Lord has opened up a whole new dimension of Madonna House — a dimension which reaches around the world and which creates a beautiful oneness in the Lord. I am proud to say that I too am an associate member.

5

COMMUNITY TESTIMONIES

Father David May: How I came to Madonna House
I am thirty-four years old and I am a priest of Madonna House, ordained four-and-a-half years ago. I will never cease to marvel at how I came here, and how I discovered my vocation.

I grew up in the United States between 1950 and 1970. This was a turbulent era, characterised by strong economic growth and important social changes. It was, however, a personal event which marked me most strongly — my parents' divorce. This happened in 1959, after years of tension and suffering. During those long years, there were in my life two important elements which would help define my destiny; a keen sense of all human suffering, and a profound desire for God. At times, this gave me a great joy and a sense of destiny, but at other times I was overcome with the painful feeling that a real God of love would not have permitted such suffering. There was in me both compassion and despair, gentleness and bitterness, desire for commitment and fear.

I attended public schools because the Catholic schools were both too expensive and too far away from our mainly Protestant area. I received from the university a good dose of existentialist and sociological atheism (Marx, Durkheim, Sartre, Nietzsche, etc.) These courses stimulated my thinking while purifying my faith.

My last year at university was one of great anguish. I know that as a Christian, I professed faith in a living, resurrected Christ. However, I was not at all convinced that Jesus was truly alive. I desperately wanted to believe in him, but I could not. This inner tension was so great that one day I left everything: home, girlfriend and work, to search for a Christ who was really alive. I met a parish priest who advised me to make a retreat in a Trappist abbey located seven hundred kilometres from my area. When I arrived there, I was told that I would do much better to go to a place in Canada — where I would be able to stay longer, to pray and work. This place was called Madonna House, and it was in Combermere, Ontario.

When doubts and anguish of heart are so overwhelming, and one wants so much to find a solution, no distance is too great. I turned northwards. Since then, much has happened. It has already been thirteen years.

Two things touched me deeply at Madonna House: the priests, in their homilies, spoke of Jesus truly alive; and the community, with its fixed rhythm of work and prayer, gave me the necessary freedom and an atmosphere that was favourable to searching, to prayer, and to a life of faith. I was like an ailing plant under the warm rays of a healing sun. This 'sun' was nothing less than the sincere, incarnated love of a family of men and women dedicated to God. Several years later, the Lord answered the quest of my childhood: I discovered Jesus at the heart of my own suffering. This Jesus spoke to me peacefully but firmly: 'Like you, David, I was innocent when suffering touched me'.

Since that time, I have known that I myself, the poor and wounded young man that I was, have resurrected with Him.

It was this that Madonna House has meant to me: a group of people, poor and without pretensions — like Mary — who marvel to see themselves brought back to life with the Lord, whose name is Jesus: eternal joy and salvation.

Miriam Stulberg: The place where I could find God. . .
Born in Detroit, Michigan in 1947, I first heard of Madonna House while was in high school. Although I came from a Jewish family and lived in a Jewish suburb of Detroit, I was an agnostic at the time. Our family was what might be called 'cultural Jews'. We identified ourselves as Jews, and we celebrated the major Jewish feasts, but in the context of the liberal and pluralistic American society, we had rejected the religious orthodoxy and ghetto mentality of my immigrant grandparents' generation. Nevertheless, I had continued to search for God, and for the meaning of my life. I belonged to the sixties' generation and I soon found myself involved in the protest movements of that era: human rights, the war against poverty, and the opposition to the Vietnam War.

After finishing university, I had gone to Boston, which at that time was a hotbed of radical American Catholicism. It was here that I met a number of nuns and priests who were deeply committed to the peace movement. I was doing social work at the time, and I began to find in the Catholic Church (such as it was interpreted to me by my friends) a source of meaning for my work. For the first time in my life, I realised clearly that my own life would only have meaning in terms of the life of the rest of humanity. Little by little, I began to understand my relationship to other people in terms of the life of Jesus Christ himself.

I began to be more and more involved in politics. The activists of my generation ran the risk of arrest and jail sentence. I began to ask myself what was my real goal — what was I really looking for in all this political and social involvement? I had stayed in contact with the high school teacher who had first spoken to me of Madonna House, and I had read Thomas Merton's autobiography, *The Seven-Story Mountain*, in which I recognised the 'Baroness' as the 'Catherine' of whom my teacher had spoken. What had struck me more than anything was this teacher's description of 'young people who were happy!' I didn't know anyone among my generation who was really happy. Everyone I knew was searching, anguished, neurotic, on drugs — but *happy*? My friends all assured me that Madonna House was much too old-fashioned, much too traditional, and that I wouldn't like it at all. But something was pushing me to go, find out for myself. I had already quit my job, and was only too happy to get out of the city which had become for me a symbol of human suffering and meaninglessness.

Having written to Combermere, I bought a bus ticket and left with the intention of spending a weekend there, in the country. (I stayed for eight months.) It was a night bus, and as we sped down the highway, the headlights piercing the darkness of the road before us, I found myself thinking, 'This is what my life is like. . . I can see the light just in front of me, but I have no idea where it is leading. . .'

At Madonna House, I was welcomed with warmth, simplicity, and love. It utterly disarmed me. In Boston, I had discovred Christ in a world of material misery; in Combermere, I found him in my own interior poverty. I knew I had to let go of my self-image, my mask, my role-playing, to drop my presuppositions. I had thought I was looking for a political commitment, but now I began to understand that what I really had been looking for was God. It went without saying that I had many ambitions and dreams of the future. But something within me insisted: 'You can travel all over the world, but what you are looking for is here. Stay still and dig deeply.'

I had asked Catherine if I might stay on at Madonna House.

She advised me to return to the States in order to get to know my Jewish roots. It made sense, but I could only stammer, 'but — what about Jesus?' and she understood.

What had struck me and moved me so strongly at Madonna House, was the fact I had been welcomed and accepted for myself, and with a particular love and respect because of the fact that I was Jewish. The more I came to know Catherine, the more I began to realise what it meant to be Jewish. I never felt at Madonna House the slightest pressure to become a Catholic; on the contrary, the community encouraged me to come to know my own past, my roots, my Jewish culture. One of the greatest gifts of Madonna House to me has been the discovery of the depth of this inner identity.

On 21 December 1969 I was baptised in the Madonna House Chapel, after a catechumenate in which the whole community had participated. I left Madonna House some months later and found a job, but returned the following year. At this point, there was no longer the exhilaration of newness and discovery. Christianity was no longer synonymous with community life, and various attractive alternatives were available to me. I had neither the interest nor the desire to live a life of poverty, chastity and obedience! But a well had opened up within my being. Its depth called out to me and I could not ignore its presence.

Finally, some weeks after my return to Madonna House, my spiritual director suggested I go to the poustinias. 'Don't think', he said, 'just write'. I followed his advice. On a sheet of paper, I listed my reasons for staying and reasons for leaving. They balanced each other out. I continued to write and I found myself writing the following words: 'I cannot live without God. If I truly want him, this is the place where I can hear him.' Suddenly, there was deep peace in my heart. If I truly wanted God, it was here, in this place, that I could find him.

'If you want to be perfect, sell all that you have and come follow me', said Christ, looking insistently at the rich young man. I heard his words, and I knew that they were addressed to me.

This was the birth of my Madonna House vocation. I have never doubted it since.

Father Emile Briere: The essentials at Madonna House
The essentials at Madonna House: The formulation and development of these go back to 1962 when rebellious youth, clergy and nuns began to visit us. Faced with this onslaught,

Catherine, Father Cal and myself asked: 'What do we centre our lives upon at this moment of real crisis in the Catholic Church?' and our answer was: 'The essentials.' That is, God is love. God loves you. God is Father, Son and Holy Spirit. God revealed himself and became man in Jesus Christ. Each one of us can live out the various phases of the life of Jesus at one time or another and perhaps often within the space of a few hours, such as Bethlehem — its helplessness; Nazareth — its wealthy, rich, productive hiddenness, in the doing of simple things. (You will never go wrong by following Nazareth. It will leave a glow upon your face that will preach to our visitors more strongly than anything else.) You live his public life, when you teach, when you listen; his passion, his death and resurrection, when you undergo in your own heart, soul and flesh, the totally frightening darkness, helplessness and torture of his passion and death, and the glory of his resurrection. All this within the mantle of Our Lady of Combermere, trusting in her no matter what. Trusting that she takes care of you in every situation; takes care of your house; takes care of Madonna House, no matter what.

We realised twenty-two years ago that the extremely sophisticated opinions which were being expressed by various theologians could only lead to the total confusion of the people of God. And so we determined with all of our hearts to stress the essentials of love, of the Trinity, the Incarnation, the Passion and the death and resurrection of Jesus, the presence of the Holy Spirit and of Mary, in all of our lives to such an extent that people could find direction — re-direction for their lives; could rediscover faith; could again place their trust in God, in Jesus the Lord, in Our Lady and escape the confusion.

A family like Madonna House is created by the Holy Spirit and Our Lady. They call us to this way of life. They give us the vocation and each person is carefully chosen. It does not take long to realise that people have different weaknesses and different strengths. One person's gift will carry the other one's problem. Community is not made of people who are the same. What are your strengths, your special gifts from God for this family? What are your weaknesses which your brothers and sisters are asked to carry — to help you carry? What are the strengths, the special gifts of the staff workers you associate with? Competitiveness is an enemy of love and community. When people recognise each other's gifts, they do not have to compete and they can begin benefitting from each other's gift while carrying each other's weakness. It is our arrogance, our self-sufficiency, that has to be broken until we trust fully in God and in others, until we depend entirely upon God and upon our family. Then we become strong, each one personally and the family as a whole. Each one of us is a part of the Body of Christ, of His mystical or mysterious Body. (*1 Cor 12:12-20*)

Mariann Dunsmore: An oasis of hospitality

I was born in Toronto in 1956. Like my four sisters, I was baptised and confirmed in the Catholic Church, but without receiving real instruction in that faith. After finishing high school, I worked for a while in order to save enough money to travel for a year to Europe. As I left home, I was moved to go into a church for Confession and Communion.

At the end of a year, I returned to Canada again to get enough money together to leave for Israel, to work there in a kibbutz. I was, however, both disappointed and bitter at finding there so little sense of real unity or love of neighbour. It was as if we lived enclosed in a narrow mentality.

I had heard about Mother Teresa of Calcutta and set out for India with my wealth of one hundred dollars.

Asia brimmed over with life. There I saw, for the first time in my life, how Moslems prayed in the street, and how the poor brought their offerings to little shrines along the road. Everything there was as if it were impregnated with the odour and beauty of God, and I was painfully aware of what was lacking in my own culture.

My parents had given me the name and address of a Jesuit brother in Darjeeling, so I decided to visit him. I arrived there on Christmas Eve. Rather abruptly, Brother Mara asked me if I wanted to go to Confession. I agreed and received Holy Communion also. I experienced very closely the presence of God. During this time in Darjeeling, I met many missionaries. Their life and commitment greatly impressed me.

I returned to Calcutta to help Mother Teresa's group in work with orphans. One day I met a Canadian who asked me, right in the middle of the street, what I was looking for in India. It was then that he spoke to me about a group of men, women and priests who gave their lives to the service of the poor, and who lived at Madonna House in Combermere, south of Ottawa. I decided to go there and meet these people.

It has now been seven years since my arrival here. It was for me the discovery of the meaning and goal of my life. I stayed there to live the gospel in the midst of my own people: as an alternative to every form of injustice and man's inhumanity to man. But first, I had to live out this alternative in the depth of my heart, where I was able to discover, after a long inner journey, Jesus and his Gospel. Madonna House is an oasis of hospitality. I ask the Lord in prayer for the ability to help all those who pass through to experience God, the Beloved, in this house where we live and work to serve and love others.

Father Robert Wild: 'You kind of hold people before God in your heart.'

Living in the poustinia for me has meant trying to pray from the heart. This means many things.

The poustinia give you a deeper sense of intercessory prayer. You feel impelled to carry people in your heart, but you don't necessarily feel like 'saying prayers' for them. That's not quite it. You just kind of hold them before God, in your heart. That is intercessory prayer.

The prayer of the heart means descending through the layers of all your emotional hang-ups, and facing them. You have to quit being a child (as St Paul says).

It means, then, that you begin to really see your own moral failings and sins — pride, anger, lust. These are not simply your emotional reactions but the actual sicknesses in the heart. You have to face it all and not despair. What begins to grow from this is the spirit of repentance, and true mourning and compunction for sin. I pray constantly for this gift of spiritual weeping because I think it's one of the things the poustinik is called to do: weep for the sins of the world.

This gift too is far removed from surface emotional weeping. It's an inward weeping, a fruit of prayer and penance. You sense a kind of weeping yourself; yes, a weeping for your own sins, but it expands and includes the sins of others and of the whole world.

It's not self-centred weeping beause you don't measure up to your ego ideal. It may begin there, but eventually you mourn over God, over the sufferings of Christ which somehow continue in his Body. Billions of people do not know Christ; billions of people are in spiritual danger. You realise that God's plan for so many people is not being realised. In a way you try to identify with the woman who wept over Christ's feet at the banquet. This weeping is a fruit of the prayer of the heart.

The Eastern tradition speaks also about the cleansing power of tears. It washes your eyes so you can look with tenderness and compassion on all creatures. If you realise in your heart you are a sinner, you are merciful towards others.

The poustinia teaches simplicity. Your relationship with others, and the way you relate to the world, becomes more a matter of the heart than the head. The word 'heart' in our culture also has strong emotional connotations. I don't mean this. The heart is the centre of the person where all volitional, knowing forces come together, and you 'know' with your being, not just with one part of you.

To sum it up, you might say that the poustinia leads one to the centre of his being. To get there, all the emotional, merely intellectual/abstract powers — the powers which often build towers of Babel within — these noises are stilled. Then with the 'heart' one can really hear the Word of God. To hear this Word is our true life.

Rejeanne George: Journey to the heart of Jesus

My grandparents emigrated to western Canada from the Franco-Belgian border at the turn of the century on one of the last great waves of emigration. It was there, in the little town of Bellegrade, Saskatchewan, that I was born and grew up, then went on to become a teacher. I made my first promises in the community of Madonna House on 15 August 1957.

In each life there are moments of grace which are like lights that illuminate our path to God. Even today, I can see clearly the origins of my vocation to Madonna House. A birth that was not without pain, as any birth is wont to be, brought me into a fullness of life such as I had never expected and which remains the source of that life.

Children sometimes have a vision of the realities of life which can be astounding. I vividly recall such a moment in my life as a child. I was bending over the cot of the youngest at home — a beautiful child. He was asleep, a deep peace and contentment written all over his features. It was such a contrast to what I felt in my own heart which was full of a pain I could not understand. Bitter tears silently coursed down my cheeks. Suddenly, I understood something: pain can be the source of life and understanding providing it is borne without rancour;

pain can give birth to compassion and understanding and give one a heart of flesh. That for me was a moment of grace — I treasured it in my child's heart.

As I moved into adolescence, it gave me a kind of call to befriend those who felt lonely and unpopular. Little by little I became conscious that therein lay my life's calling and that in order to live it out in its fullest, mine was a vocation to celibacy. It was a choice made much easier by the extraordinarily mature love of a young medical student who said to me one day, 'Rejeanne, I love you too much to stand in the way of what seems to be your vocation'.

I thought of entering traditional religious life but somehow knew that that was not my calling any more than it was to live a single life in the world. It was a time of great uncertainty and even confusion, until one day I heard in my heart Jesus' words: 'Whoever leaves everything behind for My Name's Sake, shall receive a hundredfold. . .' At the same time, I recalled a visit I had made with a group of Young Christian Farmers to a place in the backbush of Ontario. It was called Madonna House. Its foundress was Catherine Doherty. What had struck me so powerfully there was a sense of 'family', something I had never touched in any religious house before. Equally striking for me was the fact that the men and women who lived there were lay people living simply among the people of the area, sharing their lives, even while taking simple promises of poverty, chastity and obedience.

I decided to go there for three weeks. Five months later I was still there, and face-to-face with a decision to be made: was this my vocation? I prayed and struggled. On the eve of 8 December it became very clear: here, in this house of Our Lady, was where the deepest desires of my heart would be fulfilled. Here at Madonna House with its life of simplicity and ordinariness, with its call to be 'one with the poor', to 'pray always', to 'listen to the spirit', my being would find the home of its heart. I have been in this community since 1956.

My journeying, my appointments, the time I have spent in Ottawa and Moncton here in Canada, in Honduras in Central America, in the state of Michigan in the United States, as well as now in France and England are all part of that interior journeying to which we are all called: that journey to the heart of Jesus who is the Way, the Truth and the Life.

Karen van de Loop: It starts with Jesus

I was seventeen years old and walking home from school in a small town in a northern state. Jesus spoke a deep word of love to me right there on the crumbling tar of 5th Street in front of Peg Pagel's house. There was an out-of-the-ordinariness about the moment and I knew Jesus was speaking to me. I stopped walking and talked with Him. After years of hinting, he clearly came out with it and asked me to follow Him — Him alone.

As youth often is, I was in love with everyone and everything. I told Jesus I would follow Him if it meant He would love me as intimately as a husband would.

He said, YES, He would. Jesus promised me He would always love me — intimately. He said that is what following Him is all about.

So, I said YES, too.

I only knew one thing to do: love. Nuns love Jesus. I would be a nun. I greatly needed clear, spiritual guidance at this point. I timidly looked for, and received little encouragement, for I was the 'wild one'.

Determining things of my own, I knew only one thing to do. I could see that IT had to be done in secret so I would not be recognised, refused, and humiliated. I would go quietly into a convent.

The decision with which I struggled was full of difficulties as I straddled a line. On one side I was promised intimacy with Jesus, on the other side was the reckless abandonment to a life I loved so much.

I avoided the decisive step for three years. And then I stepped forward, begged for, and accepted the habit of St Francis of Assisi.

The next sixteen years I spent as a Franciscan Sister were good years. I taught with this congregation of fine women whom I loved. Our mother house was in Milwaukee, Wisconsin.

I prayed and I studied theology. I was gratifyingly successful in my professional work. It seemed enough. But it never was enough. In the quiet hours I always heard: Jesus alone. Did anyone else hear those words? I became ruthless, restless for whom I could never really say. I had lost touch with my true vocation of intimacy with Jesus. My insides were churning with a passion to set things right with me.

My nature is a rebellious one; I kicked up my heels as I quite blindly sought my lost coin. My long-suffering Franciscan sisters had to ride out a great deal of squally weather with me.

My prayer wearied; Jesus, ever merciful, heard it.

Now I was not a naive seventeen-year-old on 5th Street. I was a somewhat sophisticated principal of a poor school on Chicago's all black south side. I had a lot to give but I used it all up and was left with nothing — emotionally, physically, psychologically and spiritually. I was sick. I was exhausted. I was close to despair. And where was Jesus in my life?

Then came the summer of 1969. After that spring of rioting in our city of Chicago, my spirit was sore. Quite by accident, one of those coincidences we call miracles, I came to Madonna House for the first time. My plan was that I would stay five weeks and then go to summer school, furthering my studies in school administration.

Catherine Doherty's Madonna House in Combermere presented an essence that I understood and it penetrated through to my bones. No part of me escaped the saving power of my God. And the word he spoke was: Karen, you have come home!

In a practical way I did what had to be done. I worked hard, prayed, fought black flies, swam in the river, discovered Byzantine spirituality, made friends, got a spiritual director.

For five weeks I repented, repented, repented. Lord have mercy on me a sinner. The Little Mandate was emblazoned on my heart. I heard the Gospel preached as for the first time — the Good News. My Franciscan vocation solidified and was being fulfilled in the form of this little group tucked off in the woods. I found my lost coin. I was coming around full circle.

I had come home and I felt God was changing my vocation. Shyly I told B of all this. What should I do?

I may not have known exactly what to do, but not B! 'Wait five years. Stay where you are. Keep doing what you are doing. God will let us know what to do', she said: I agreed.

I had arrived in Combermere in an exhausted state. The intensity of the conversion I experienced increased that. There was no summer school for me that year. Three days after I returned to Chicago I was admitted to a hospital. My admission card said: 'suspected lymphoma'. I'm told I nearly died. The medical staff did not know that that is exactly what was happening. I was dying. It was a death to all within me that had to die. Jesus was continuing His loving teaching in my heart. How receptive I was in those days of weakness! He enlightened my mind and encouraged me with truth; Jesus told me in His heart and consoled me with His mercy.

Medically the diagnosis was negative, and my body healed up enough so that four months later a transformed Karen returned to her principal's office at Our Lady of Solace School. Our Lady had been my comfort.

The advice that had been given me was to stay with my original decision. Don't keep making it over again for the next five years. Live and let God do what He would do.

I tried to let go of arranging and directing the movements of my heart. I had successful months of calmly hearing God's word, times of loving repair of my heart. And I was brought low by a number of miserable failures during the wait, some lengthy periods of dismal unfaithfulnes.

As the end of the five-year waiting period came into view I knew one thing certainly: I did not know what God wanted me to do. He had not spoken. I could see no light on the horizon. My own light failed me. For some months I barely left my room, seldom went to Mass or community prayers. I lost my job, ignored my friends. Where was God? I rebelled against His power. I never prayed.

Seeing this distress and trying to touch the blackness I was in, a good friend asked me one evening what I hoped for. A silence came instead of an answer and then it lengthened. I began to feel a cold stricture in my stomach. I saw I had hope in nothing. Was this despair? Despair of God finishing what He had begun, would He never speak?

From that night on, my friend did for me what I could not do. She came to my room each morning and we went to the Eucharist; she saw that I ate food; and I again met each night with all my sisters and we prayed. They quietly held me before God. I dumbly responded with an aching desire to be broken open, to be a lover again, to be forgiven. I could only manage to hold the Eucharist in my heart and weep, to gaze with emptiness on my Crucified Jesus, to sigh before the icon of Mary.

Holy Week was coming; I went to Combermere for it and asked God to settle with me while I was there. As Holy Week progressed, my darkness wasn't altered. Nothing was happening. The only inner movement was that the pain of separation from Jesus grew with the ceremonies of each day. I was ready to return home to the States, continue with my old life and forget about Madonna House for good.

Easter Monday dawned cold and rainy, no different from the way I knew life to be. Alone, I went for a long walk, praying that God's mercy would fall on me just as the rain was gently falling. I prayed the Jesus Prayer as I walked: mercy, mercy, sorrow, sorrow.

Jesus had mercy. I suddenly knew the waiting was over. I was to come to Madonna House. I was free to leave the Franciscans. Whatever God wanted me to do there was finished. I was free to go. I knew with certainty. I was at peace — great peace. I could again breathe. I would come to Madonna House to stay.

I talked with Mrs Doherty. She said, 'Good! Leave your Franciscans and come back here to see what God wants.' She promised me that I would be getting a much harder life than the one I was leaving. The decision was agreeable to my Franciscan family. They were happy to see me at peace with them and with God. The last permission to be obtained was from Rome; I was dispensed from my vows with no difficulty. I was free to join the lay apostolate of Madonna House as a personal fulfilment of my Franciscan vocation.

Francis's life was lived out in an intimacy with Jesus never before known to man, culminating in the stigmata. Catherine Doherty's strange love affair with the Cross of Jesus was familiar ground to a Franciscan. There were other parallels: love of Church; a passion for unity within the Church and between East and West; again passion for poverty, childlikeness, simplicity and meekness. There was the great love and confidence in the Mother of God: Our Lady of the Angels for Francis and the Bogoroditza for Catherine.

My part in this process had been haltingly faithful and filled with painful detours. Nearly one year after arriving at Madonna House, I left it. Yes, after this pained search, I left. Even though I had found my way, I broke down from the rigour of the journey. Despondently, I departed.

Again there were months of the unendurable agony of abandonment and the struggle of facing that I had deeply failed my God. Mercifully the weeks passed, and the hidden, healing balm of the desert cleansed me and edged me into the silence of my heart, there to find His rest. Jesus and His mother brought me back into the heart of the family. I returned to Madonna House to 'learn of Jesus who is meek and humble of heart', to love Him intimately even though I knew I would fail Him over and over again, and to welcome all He would do to gather me into His heart.

This year, nearly thirty years after first accepting Jesus' invitation to be loved intimately by him, I took my final promises as a Madonna House staff worker — to live the Gospel without compromise according to the *Little Mandate* forever.

Often in the summer I like to go boating down our Madawaska River to a widening spot where the current is slow. I lie back in the boat and see on every horizon the overlapping hills of pine and rock. You see the hills only; they fill your eyes.

My heart fills. 'Jesus, you are the desire of the everlasting hills. You are the God who is my faithful lover. You have pursued me down the labyrinthine ways of my mind.'

> You come leaping on the mountains,
> bounding over the hills.
> I hear my Beloved.
> See how he comes.
> (*Song of Songs 2:8*)

Father Emile Briere: A unique saint in the history of the Church

Catherine is a very unique saint in the history of the Church. For many years she blew up easily at people for one reason or another, for one statement or another they had made. Her vision of the truth, of reality, was so great that the proposition held out to her seemed so totally incongruous with the reality in which she lived that she could blow up. Her favourite expressions were: 'Don't you see? Can't you see? It's so simple.' But most of all, she was — and is — passionately involved in the love of Jesus, of the Father, of the Son, of the Holy Spirit. 'We have lived between heaven and earth', she would say. 'We have not lived in heaven because of the pain in our hearts; we have not lived on earth because of the hope and faith and joy and love in our hearts, but betwixt and between. Where is Madonna House? In between heaven and earth. Why should we be so fortunate, so lucky? Why should this happen to you? You may say, 'This life is just about impossible, and I was thinking of getting out of it.' We are all with you, but yet look at those trees, at the river, at the person next to you, look at your own heart and say: 'Where would I find God and happiness and joy and immense pain, but worthwhile, except here? Love is our vocation. If we look at B, what do we see all through her life, except a passionate love for God? And now, at this stage of her life, a child-like expression of love to people. Like a child she accepts love from each one of us. Our hearts have been wounded by the lances of love. Each person has the right to express to B his love in his own way and to receive her love in his own way. The gift of the Holy Spirit to Madonna House this year, 1984, is the gift of mutual, brotherly, sisterly love.

The B has taught us all her life how to love. Now she is teaching us how to receive love. Love from each person is precious, life-giving, worthy of acceptance.

from Catherine's Hermitage — 16 July 1984

6

EXCERPTS FROM THE WRITINGS OF CATHERINE DOHERTY

To live for poor, the Beloved. . .

It matters not if we are many in number, that our shelves groan under books, that we have an army of nurses rendering services to all the sick, that we live to feed the poor, unless our hearts are filled with the charity of Christ and we burn with the zeal of bringing that charity, whose other name is love, we are like sounding brass. And nothing that we do, registers. No restoration follows, only an extension of things Communists do and Pagans do these days and social workers do. The difference between us and them, is MOTIVATION. WE DO IT BECAUSE WE CANNOT HELP DOING IT. . . BECAUSE, LIKE A PERSON ON FIRE, WE MUST SERVE, BECAUSE OTHERWISE OUR LOVE OF GOD WILL SIMPLY TEAR US APART!!!! AND BECAUSE ANY LOVE SERVES.

Love is not an abstract thing. Love is not something that you can classify, weigh, organise. Love is a fire. . . it must spend itself in service. Service is the dry wood to love that makes it into a bonfire that reaches out to eternity and burns there. WHAT YOU AND I HAVE TO BE IS A FLAME in this Stygian darkness, utter darkness of this world. A lamp to my neighbour's feet. A place where he can warm himself, his hands, a place where he can see the face of God, for how can a man see in darkness? IT IS TO BE. . . TO LOVE. . . TO BURN. . . THAT WE HAVE COME TOGETHER! And Who brought us? The Fire of Love, the Holy Ghost. Little flames, coming together, each growing, uniting in various patterns, according to the call of God as expressed by the bishop. LOVING! BURNING! OFFERING OURSELVES UP IN HOLOCAUST! 'It is I who burns, Lord, consume. . . take no notice of me, in the sense of my weaknesses and my difficulties. Shape me unto Your Likeness.'

Catherine de Hueck Doherty, 22 March 1956, Staff Letter no. 140, 'The Spirit of Madonna House Apostolate'.

What is Prayer?

PRAYER is an answer
>and takes a thousand postures
>in a minute —
>bouncing,
>lifting arms in supplication. . .
>to prostration.

PRAYER is the fantastic movement
>of a dancer
>but also a person very still,
>stonelike and utterly immobile
>lost in regions that few men
>reach but many desire to.

PRAYER is a child bubbling like a brook
>words that fall open like ripe
>nuts from the lips of old
>people or anyone in between
>childhood and old age —
>the words of men, women and children
>who know God and so easily
>talk to Him!
>Their words change into
>beautiful little songs when
>they reach God.

PRAYER is a bride
>clad in sumptuous garments
>awaiting her lover.

PRAYER is a prostitute lying in the mire.

PRAYER is the calloused hands
>of the hard-working man
>reposing on his lap, aged by
>overwork.

PRAYER is a cry of a child
>born in the slums of Calcutta
>or any other slums.

PRAYER is the clear voice of a village
>being surrounded by bulldozers.

PRAYER is the sound of brooks and rivers
and nature as it brings
suffering from the intrusion of man.
And it is the sound of brooks
and rivers and nature when it
is left alone by men to the
glory of God.

PRAYER is all people and all things
lying on earth. All these
merge, blending somewhere,
someplace into two hands, the
tip of each finger touching
the tip of Another Hand.

PRAYER is two leafy branches
touching Another
somewhere in the cosmos —
Two moons and a thousand suns
lifting their rays
and encompassing the stars,
each with folded hands
(that are not hands at all).
each blending into the folding.

That is what prayer is.

A prayer to the most holy Trinity

Doxology
I have been meditating for a long time on this short beautiful
prayer: 'Glory be to the Father, to the Son and to the Holy Spirit.
As it was in the beginning, is now and ever shall be. Amen.'
To me it is one of the most beautiful of all prayers. I often say
it through the day. I love it whenever it comes at Mass and the
Breviary hours; for it is the prayer, par excellence for man —
to render glory to the Triune God, One and Eternal. Every time
I say it or hear it I feel like prostrating myself, flat on my face. . .
for how else can man glorify God in such a prayer? I love to
worship, and with my body.

Glory to the Father. . .
What beautiful words! What other words express God so well,

for He is glory! Your glory, O God, is light ineffable. . . peace in my soul.

It is in the winds of all seasons and all songs.
It is in the whisper of earth and trees,
Herbs and all plants, small or immense.

It is in the voice of men, women and children
Who know you and adore you.
Each according to the knowledge
You gave them.

It is in all creation everywhere
To be seen and adored everywhere
By a heart overflowing with awe
and love.

Your glory is in your love of man
Your steps on earth,
Your cry on the cross
Your silence in the tomb
And in the bread and wine.

Your glory is even in me, a sinner!

I adore and glorify and worship
You,
My Lord and my God,
Loving you beyond all loves.

The Father
It seems to me I will faint just hearing or trying to pronounce this beautiful word — You, the Lord Almighty, 'OUR FATHER'. Each letter of that word speaks, sings, thunders of love. . . It tastes of love, of light, of joy, of complete security. Honey is bitter compared to its taste.

This word fills the soul with such gladness that I can scarcely bear it. . . Like a furnace, a fire burns in my soul, warming me forever.
F...A...T...H...E...R! O GOD, I love You! I adore You! I glorify You! For you are my Father. I belong to you, Your daughter!!! Of Your household. I have access to You always, as a child to its father. Your house is my house.

O God, truly my spirit faints for it cannot encompass this thought. I can only stand before it and sing Your Glory.

The Son
You, my beloved Lover, Brother and God.
   You who showed me the Father.
   You who paid the price of bringing me home
   Into His loving arms.

O Jesus, O Christ, O Son of the Father
   My Brother, my love and my Lover,
   My Saviour, my God!

I love You, I adore You, I desire You.
   I worship You.
   I am all Yours, Son of the Father!

The Holy Spirit
Spirit of Love, wind of grace,
   Knowledge,
A thousand gifts and graces.
You alone know my love for you.
Crimson Dove of love
Bringing love, being loved.
Singing love, teaching love.
O my Crimson Dove, how can I thank you?
How can I spend my life adoring You?
Making You known and loved, O Holy Spirit?

Beauty unsurpassed, fire and flame,
Guide, teacher,
Wind of love, lift me up so that I
May dissolve myself in You
Who too are One.

As it was in the beginning
   Is always
   Now
   And ever shall be.
You have no beginning,
   Only we have.
But eternity is truly Your
   Footstool,
And this prayer brings it to us
   That we may climb on it
Like little children that we are
   To get into Your arms.

O I love this prayer
  With a great love! Amen.

Loneliness

Dark as the night
is the pain of Christ.
Dark as the night
and as lonely.
Strange as the night
is the silence of Christ. . .
and as deep.
Long as the night
is the suffering of Christ. . .
Long as the night. . .
and as endless!

Day stands outside of it
crouching and fearful. . .
For once it seems
it cannot conquer the night!
For the night holds
the pain of Christ. . .
holds his pains and his tears,
holds his joy,
and will not let go.

Chalice of night,
will you reveal
to a loving heart
the sight of the one tear,
the echo of one sigh,
the one cry of pain,
so that it might
wipe the tears,
share the pain,
and gather the sighs
like an endless refrain?

But the night stands still,
recollected,
holding all of it

unto herself.
For even she will not
give away
the secret of the
king of kings.

There is but one way
for a loving heart
it must enter the night
and weep where he wept,
and sigh where he sighed
and suffer his pain.

Will you open
the door of your heart,
dark night,
for a loving heart?
The door is unlocked,
and the loving heart
now abides
in the heart of the night
that holds it tight
but allows it to move
in the breadth and the width
of this endless night
that held his torment.

It takes in
all the nights of time
that waited
for this night of nights,
this night
that held
Gethsemani.

Will you lift her up,
dark night, the loving heart,
and let her in. . .

Lift her up
and let her cover him
from the sight of men?
It cannot be done.
He has to hang

naked and lone
on the tree of death
like a king on a throne,
with naught but the night at noon
to cover his shame.

The loving heart stands
at the foot of the cross,
shrouded in the warm noon-night.
She cannot see a thing.
But the warmth of His blood,
she feels,
falling to the earth.
And some of it brushes her
as it falls
and she knows ecstasy.
As she does the night.

Strong as the night
is the pain of Christ,
and as deep.
And why shouldn't it be?
For the night gathered up the pain
and kept it in the chalice
of the dark. . .
And all who seek Him
must walk to his light
through the dark of the night.

What is a Priest?

A PRIEST is a lover of God,
a priest is a lover of men,
a priest is a holy man
because he walks before the face of the All-Holy.

A priest understands all things
A priest forgives all things,
A priest encompasses all things.

The heart of a priest is pierced,
like Christ's with the lance of love.

The heart of a priest is open,
like Christ's for the whole world to walk through.

The heart of a priest is a vessel of compassion,
the heart of a priest is a chalice of love,
the heart of a priest is the trysting place of human
    and divine love.

A priest is a man whose goal is to be another Christ;
a priest is a man who lives to serve.

A priest is a man who has crucified himself so that he too
may be lifted up and draw all things to Christ.

A priest is a man in love with God.

A priest is the gift of God to man and of man to God.

A priest is the symbol of the Word made flesh,
a priest is the naked sword of God's justice,
a priest is the hand of God's mercy,
a priest is the reflection of God's love.

Nothing can be greater in this world than a priest,
nothing but God himself.

Don't desert us!

In the past I have written books entitled *Dear Bishop*, *Dear Seminarian* and *Dear Sister*. I love bishops, seminarians and religious but not exactly in the same way that I love you, God's priests, who are charged with the daily spiritual care of God's people. It is because of my special love for you that I have waited so long to put down in book form my feelings for you. My love for you and respect for your special ministry has deepened and grown throughout my life.

Long ago, when I was about eleven or twelve, and far away in a convent of the Sisters of Sion in Ramleh near Alexandria, Egypt, a Jesuit priest gave us little ones a talk. He was holy and simple. He touched my young heart deeply. However, I didn't like it when he asked us to 'pray for priests when we became a little more grown up'. I asked myself, 'Why should I wait an eternity — until I reach eighteen or nineteen — to pray for priests?' I spoke privately with the priest and explained my longing to pray for priests at once.

The Jesuit looked intently and earnestly at me and asked if I truly desired to pray for priests. When I responded affirmatively, he placed his hand upon my head and prayed to the Trinity, patted my cheek and said, 'Now, I have blessed you so that, as young as you are, you can pray for priests. Don't forget to do so, child!'

I have never forgotten that special blessing. Even as a child, I loved priests with my whole heart. In my youthful mind, I firmly believed that Christ left us priests because he didn't want to leave us orphans or to part from us. I didn't understand a great deal about the Mystical Body and the many ways Christ remains in our midst. However, I sensed the very special role that priests played in Christ's plan and I found it terribly important to pray for them.

Since the age of twelve, therefore, I have continued to pray for priests. Except for the period when I, with my family, was fleeing the Communist revolution and I was too sick and weak to pray (weighing barely eighty-two pounds), I have acted upon the blessing given to me in Egypt so many decades ago.

I have stored up many things in my heart and many feelings which for so long I was hesitant or afraid to express. Before Vatican II, there were many sentiments and thoughts that one simply wouldn't think of expressing. Now, however, at the age of seventy-seven, I am not afraid, as I was in my youth, to face you, my priests, and share with you my heart.

I have actually written this book a thousand times over in my mind and heart. Yes, even now as I attempt to write it out I doubt that I will be able to convey to you my love for the priesthood and for each one of you priests of God.

Though it is difficult to write about my personal love for you, I must try. It is important for us, the laity, to communicate to you dear Fathers, both our feelings and our needs. In this book, which I visualise as letters written to you, I will convey to you the need we laity have of being guided by our shepherds. We long to hear your voices echoing the call of the one shepherd you represent so tangibly for us. If we do not hear his voice through you, how shall we hear it? Lately, your reassuring voices have either been muted or simply drowned out by the din of a noisy and confused world. We need to hear your voices clearly and we need to hear them now. Our pastures, once so green and nourishing for us, are being scorched by the searing heat of materialism, selfishness, and doubt. Only your voices united with the voice of Good Shepherd can lead us to verdant fields once again. The Prince of Darkness is clouding minds, frightening the flock, forcing us to huddle together, uncertain of the direction we must travel in.

But in the present twilight, we the laity are confident that in the face of danger, dear Fathers, you will stand by us and lead us.

At Madonna House, we insist on addressing priests as 'Father'. Though some prefer to be called simply by their first name we find it impossible to comply with their wish. We recognise too clearly the fact that the priest provides for his spiritual family as surely as a father for his natural family. A natural father is the 'breadwinner'. A priest is a 'bread giver' in the Eucharist. As we begin to learn something about God the Father's love for us through experiencing our own father's love for our own family, we learn even more about God's paternal love through your own love of all families. Thus we call you 'Father'.

A father is a man who has begotten children. He has a family he must look after. He must provide for the necessities of food, shelter, clothing, education and medical care. He must be present to his family and give them all his love, care and attention. A father is the head of a community of love. Together with his wife, he forms an atmosphere of love conducive not only to healthy human growth but to spiritual growth as well. By example, a father preaches his loudest sermons and teaches his greatest lessons. It is from his own tender, responsible actions that his children learn the heart and art of loving. Though loving his own family above all others, a father is also aware of the needs of his neighbours as well. In fact, according to his state in life and concrete situation, a father is concerned with the needs of the whole world. In all cases, however, a truly loving father is willing to submit his own needs to those of others. This is the ideal we, the laity, have of fathers.

We call you 'Father' because you begot us in the mystery of a tremendous love affair between you and God. Because you participate in the one priesthood of Christ. You are wedded to the Church, his bride. Even should the law of celibacy be rescinded, you will still be wedded to the Church, and it still will have to take precedence over everything in your life.

We call you 'Father' and we are your 'family'. We need you desperately. We need you where God has placed you, at the head of our family, just as he has placed human fathers in the midst of their families to nurture and love them.

Whenever an ordinary, human father abandons his family to fulfil his own immediate needs, he creates a truly tragic situation. His entire family, especially his children, are left confused, frightened and lost. The fact that so many human fathers have abandoned their duties accounts for so much of the anarchy that has befallen the world. The large number of priests who have abandoned their duties accounts for a great deal of the pain in the Church throughout the world.

Why so many priests have abandoned their spiritual families is difficult to say. Perhaps, under the pressure of changing values, they suddenly placed their 'own needs' before the needs of their family. I would never judge harshly the decision of any priest because I know the pressures and burdens priests bear and the spiritual agonies they encounter. However, remember, dear Fathers, you are not alone. Christ is with you. We your children, need you.

I would like to suggest, dear Fathers, that you meditate often on the state and plight of the laity you serve. We are young, middle-aged, or elderly. Some of us are married, some single. We are both well-educated and illiterate. We are rich and poor. However, all of us are like the grass, here today and gone tomorrow. Nevertheless, you can learn from us. Consider for a moment the situation of the father of a family. He works hard for his family to fulfil their needs. At times he dreams of greener fields opening up to him. However, if he loves his family he will not follow those dreams if they conflict with the real needs of his loved ones. As monotonous, unsatisfying and painful as this may be, loving fathers demonstrate their responsiveness to the needs of others by sticking to the task at hand. Yet, in spite of the two thousand problems that assail the family, things work out. They work out because of love and because of God.

We, the laity, call you by the awesome name, 'Father', because we see you attending to our spiritual needs. Always keep in mind that you were ordained to serve us, to feed us with the Eucharist, to heal us with anointing, to reconcile us to God and one another in penance, to witness our unions of love in marriage, to preach God's word.

We, the laity, can be healers in many fashions. We the laity can be charismatic healers, doctors, psychologists, psychiatrists and social workers. We can even be counsellors to you our priests! However, we cannot heal in the same sacramental sense that you, our priests, can heal. If you carry on your own proper healing ministry, you will inspire us, the laity, to carry God's saving word into the inner city and the suburbs, to the rich and the poor. We can do all this as long as you preach the Gospel to us and nurture us with the sacraments. We need you present to us wherever you may be assigned. We need to be taught by your patience, your kindness, your understanding and your fortitude, what it is to be a Christian.

Have mercy on us, your ordinary, monotonous, dumpy, unleavened flock! Teach us how to love. Teach us how to pray. Inflame our hearts with the desire to wash the feet of our poor brethren, to feed them love, and to preach the Gospel with our lives. Send us forth into the world everywhere — the world of poverty, hunger, misery — so that we may change it because we heard your voice 'sending us there' — the Shepherd's voice. Come with us if God appoints you to do so. Lead us, wherever he tells us. But do not desert us in order to fulfil personal ambition or your own immediate needs. Always seek to do God's will and you will fulfil your deepest needs and longings.

The endless pursuit of new lifestyles or academic degrees and recognition is not the way to priestly happiness. If you follow the voice of the Shepherd and pursue his values you will find peace. True, there will be turmoil in your life, just as there was turmoil in the life of every prophet and in the life of the Divine Master himself. Nevertheless, there will be that unshakeable tranquility that comes from knowing that you are doing God's will and not your own.

The prophets of old were seized with the desire to preach God's word, to teach his people. They emptied themselves for the sake of the people. They spent themselves in God's service meeting the needs of others. They gave up secular pursuits to dedicate themselves to the ministry of the word. Be careful, dear Fathers, not to abandon your priestly duties for worldly interests. Never be so taken up with the material aspects of your life (taking care of Church property, raising funds, etc.) that you neglect your spiritual duties. Never be so enamoured of lay lifestyles as to abandon your priesthood altogether!

You may want to do many noble deeds and accomplish many tasks. You might like to become a psychologist or a foreign missionary. But the most important question to be answered is not what you may want, but what God wants for you. If you want to become a psychologist or a foreign missionary to fulfil your own needs and not to serve others or to do the will of God, you will not be satisfied either as a priest or a person. Love is always the answer and scripture tells us that love is patient, is kind, is gentle. Love seeks to serve others and not the self.

I would like to tell you clearly, dear Father, that any overpowering urge to fulfil your own needs at the expense of the needs of your flock, your spiritual family, does not come from God. The urgent and immediate desire to change everything at once to suit your own tastes or inclinations does not spring from the eternally patient, all-loving God.

The impatience to fulfil yourself and your desires can only spring from our fallen nature or the Prince of False Promises. Perhaps, in a scientific age it seems foolish to consider the Prince of Darkness. But as I nightly pray and agonise over the problems that beset you, the priests I love so dearly, I hear, figuratively speaking, the barely audible, slithering movements of a serpent. The sound of that slithering serpent will be with us until the end of time. As long as we desire to do our own will rather than God's, that sound will haunt us. To hear that sound is frightening. However, to see some of God's priests apparently following that sound — promises that are so shallow, is even more frightening. Only the path of prayer can help us in this situation or any like it. When you bow your head in prayer and ask the Lord for guidance, dear Father, realise that you are not praying alone but countless people who rely on you are praying with and for you also.

Have you pondered the Book of Numbers? I was reading it recently. There is in it the question of the census of the tribes, and I came to the statute for the Levites: 'But the Levites are to pitch their tents around the tabernacle of the Testimony. In this way the wrath will be kept from falling on the whole community of the sons of Israel. The Levites are to be in charge of the tabernacle of the Testimony.'

A little further down I read, 'Yahweh spoke to Moses and said, ''I myself have chosen the Levites from among the sons of Israel, in place of the firstborn, those who open the mother's womb among the sons of Israel; these Levites therefore belong to me.'' '

Strangely enough, this made me think of priests. The Levites quie evidently are the 'first-born'. This statute of theirs simply expresses an ideal, it seems to me, that flowered into the Christian priesthood of today!

Have you meditated on it, my beloved Father? This is a sort

of confirmation for one who constantly thinks of the priesthood with so much love and so much tenderness and so much compassion. Obviously, the priest of today must 'pitch his tent next to the tabernacle of Testimony.' This means, according to my understanding, that he must keep his heart close to the Word of God, to the Gospel of Jesus Christ! The priest of today should remember that Word, for if he doesn't, the wrath of God is going to descend on all the people of God. No priest would wish this to happen.

It tears my soul apart, and I feel swords within me, as I think that more and more priests have left their tents, the sides flapping loudly to a wind that didn't come from heaven! The priests of today, even as the Levites of old, take the place of the first-born, in this case, Jesus Christ! Therefore, I brought with me, wherever I went, the custom of standing up for priests when they enter a room. For, in truth, each one is Jesus Christ. Yahweh said so himself when he spoke of the Levites and their role.

As my meditation continued in this strange Book of Numbers, I realised over again that the Levites (and this means also the modern priesthood) 'are his property. . . belong to him'.

Somehow, this meditation that took place one night made my prayers for priests more fervent than ever before. I was besieged with an urgency to implore the Lord to stop the leakage of priests. Everything became so tremendously clear regading the role of the priests, above all the fact that they were God's special property and hence intensely blessed by him. In his eyes they were his 'first-born' and they were to dwell near him in their tents. For what is the altar of Testimony but himself?

As the glories of the priesthood invaded my heart I cried out to the Lord, 'Lord let them see who they are. Don't let them wander away into the dark wind that doesn't come from heaven.' But all the time I also knew that God already is trying — sending his grace, his charisms, his love, giving himself to priests everywhere, but that he would never interfere with their free will, the free will he has given all of us. This is fantastic: The All-Powerful has put a restriction upon himself and limited his power so that we, the children of man, may truly be free! Incredible, isn't it?

I don't know why I am writing this to you but I think God has chosen you to live closely, very closely, to the altar of Testimony, to understand better than others that you belong to God, that you are his property, and to know daily in a great depth as time goes by, that you are his first-born. This is given to you so that you might preach it, give it, offer it, in the chalice of the tenderness of your love and compassion to other priests.

Yes, dear Father, this is a very botched-up first chapter of a book. But then, every word was torn out of my heart while I prayed one night for all the priests of the world. No one writes too well with pieces of her heart.

(*Dear Father*, New York, 1976)

7

PASS IT ON

One of her sayings I had seen posted here and there at Madonna House was: 'Pass it on'. I asked more about this saying and was told that Catherine was always saying that. Something has helped you, pass it on to someone else. In other words SHARE. We are not alone; we are members of the Body of Christ and have a responsibility to help one another in every way that we can. I too, was to share in a wonderful way which I had not anticipated. It came about in this way:

I was talking with Father John Callahan, who was at that time the Director General of the priests at Madonna House. He said: 'You have seen our peole at work in Israel. You know Catherine, and Bishop Raya is a real brother to you. If you desire to, you may join the group of associate priests. Wherever you may go or work as a priest, you can be a witness to what God is working out in the Church and in the world via Catherine and Madonna House.' I was delighted to begin my year of waiting and learning more of the spirit of Madonna House.

Thus it was that a year later the Toronto bus brought me again to Combermere. Catherine met me in the spacious dining hall. She kissed my hand and said: 'Bless me, Father. . . welcome to the family!' A few days later she announced to the family that Bishop Raya would give me the Pax Caritas cross, meaning that she had taken me in as a new priest-son in the family of Madonna House.

In the middle of the dining room, a little shrine of Mary had been erected for this occasion. Bishop Delaquis was present again and Father Callahan smiled gently as Bishop Raya, surrounded by Suzy, Mary Kay, Mary and Teresa who had returned from Haifa, placed the Madonna House cross on my neck. Catherine wore her most beautiful dress for the occasion, and a pair of earrings with Eilat stones graced her serene face.

After these contacts and meetings, I learned to know and appreciate Madonna House and its staff members more. Several times I had the privilege of conversing with Catherine about the

Church and our mission in it. I had the opportunity to listen to her story about her life and her apostolate, about God whom we can experience in the Poustinia, about 'Sobornost', the Russian term for unity of mind and heart about which Jesus spoke in the gospel and which forms the foundation of the community and family spirit at Madonna House. It is the unity with God and with people which we have to proclaim and live as 'Strannik' — pilgrims.

I had befriended John Callahan, the spiritual father of the apostolate, the man of silent presence; the priest with a great love for Mary and for the Church. I learned to know also the other priests: Robert Wild who had spent a few years in England in a Carthusian cloister, and had now decided to live the life of a Poustinik in Combermere; Emile Briere, a former professor at a seminary who had now become Catherine's secretary; Eugene Cullinane, the 'holy staretz', as Bishop Raya calls him; Bob Pelton, the academic; Bob Sharkey, a Dominican from New York, and now, too, a Poustinik; Paul Bechard, the parish priest who became a Poustinik and who is also a carpenter at Madonna House; Jim Duffy, who had been working for many years in Central and South America as active director of the mission works, and is now taking charge of the formation of the prospective priests' programme at Madonna House. Tom, David and Ron are all young priests who have become priests through Madonna House and are real brothers to one another.

When Gene Cullinane, the man who is very concerned about the Marian devotion of the priests, was leaving for a pilgrimage to Fatima, I saw him asking for a blessing from Father Briere. The latter placed a small pocket icon on his head and slowly signed him with the cross, after which they embraced each other fraternally.

Apart from the priests, I learned also to appreciate and love the non-priest staff members, men as well as women. Al Osterberger is the ex-US Air Force officer and manager of the farm. He has a keen mind and great capacity for organisation and management but has a beautiful, childlike simplicity. I learned to love Joseph, Joe, Larry, Scott, Mike and Ronnie, the farmers for God, each with his own vocation story. I met Miriam, Karen, Rejeanne, Linda, Joan, Helen, Sushi and many others whose life at Madonna House is an expression of a genuine love of God and a desire to serve him in their neighbour.

I met Janet Lukos, young and talented — a genuine artist

with hand and voice, a staff member formerly in charge of formation, now afflicted with terminal cancer. It was touching at the liturgy for the sick (which is celebrated once a month) to hear her pray:

> Grant, Lord, that all who are
> sick and find themselves near
> the valley of death, may contemplate
> the radiant splendour of Your Face.

Then she went to stand before the priest who anointed her while Mary and John laid their hands on her shoulders praying quietly. A few weeks later she went to meet her Bridegroom.

In the chapel, and in all the mission houses of Madonna House, there hangs an Image which she has modelled. It is the Infant Jesus in swaddling clothes, usually mounted on a board on which is printed (or near it) Catherine's prayer: 'Give me the heart of a child, and the awesome courage to live it out.' A short time before her death, when I went to bid her goodbye before leaving, Catherine said to me: 'Speak to me especially about hope, Father, and bless me so that I may remain courageous.'

She now lies in the small cemetery near the little white church of the Parish of Combermere. In this little cemetery along the Madawaska River, lie the first deceased of Madonna House. These include: Father Eddie Doherty, Catherine's husband and co-founder of Madonna House; Father John Callahan, Paul Lussier, Janet Lukos, Alma Beauchamp, Mary Ann Gilmore and Grace Flewelling. On the simple, wooden crosses marking their graves one can read the following inscriptions which are a summary of their lives or a prayer from the heart: 'All my Words for the Word', 'Ave Maria!' 'Pax Caritas', 'Look towards him and be radiant'.

Several times a year the whole family, praying the rosary, processes to the cemetery to pray for the brothers and sisters who now live on in 'Molchani', the silence of God.

Often while there I talked with Catherine and the priests about the spirit of Madonna House and how it is being spread. 'You must look at us', Bishop Raya had told me, 'with the eyes of the Gospel. Then you will see that God is working wonderful things here. These people here, lay people as well as priests, keep on growing in love with God and therefore of people. The time will come when still more people will pay attention to what is

111

being accomplished here — the wonderful harmony and grace of Eastern and Western Spirituality.'

And people *are* paying attention. Slowly the Madonna House spirit is becoming known and the influence of Madonna House is growing not only in the United States, but around the world. Catherine Doherty's books are read more and more in Asia and Latin America. (The Latin American Bishops have circulated the book *Poustinia* in large numbers among their priests.) The Poustinia ideal is getting a following. Missionaries are telling that Poustinias are being erected in South India, Rwanda, South Africa, Brazil and in the Caribbean Islands. They said that Catherine's spiritual message is being lived out there. Even in Western Europe Poustinias are being built. The Madonna House books, heretofore published mainly in English or perhaps French, are gradually being translated into many other languages. In the young churches and missions where English is spoken, these books are designated as sound spiritual literature and in France, England, the Netherlands and Belgium, interest in the movement is growing.

'Probably God is using our modest Madonna House and our small family to make God better known and more loved and to inspire the Church, especially the priests and the lay apostles', said Father Robert Wild, the Poustinik priest who does a lot of editing of Madonna House literature, 'but I know that in Europe this is not easy. Centuries on end you were fortunate enough to gather and preserve the treasures of the spiritual and mystical life. Yet, you can still learn something from others. . . also from what takes place on the North American continent. Here too, the Spirit is active. Is this not the meaning of mission? To give and to receive in a reciprocal relationship and to help one another to enter more deeply into the life of God himself in order to go to people.'

'Pass it on', one can read on the walls of Madonna House. To tell the story and to pass on the message of Madonna House, we wrote this book.

However, the Madonna House of Combermere, situated in the hinterland of Canada, cannot serve as a blueprint for other continents and the religious phenomenon which is taking place there has to be seen and evaluated in the light of the life history of Catherine Doherty, and has to be understood from her life, the region and the country where it mainly took place.

Catherine Doherty is a saint of this century. She can be placed side by side with other great women of the Church of our times: Mother Teresa of Calcutta, Chiara Lubich, Little Sister Madeleine of the Little Sisters of Jesus and many other admirable witnesses of God's love. In fact, several aspects of the Madonna House spirituality are found also with Mother Teresa's Missionaries of Charity, the Focolare Movement and the Foucauld spirituality groups.

One of the most successful ways the Madonna House spirit is passed on is through the field houses or mission houses of Madonna House. These are centres of concern for and the care of the bodily, materially and spiritually poor. This work takes place in close coordination with the local ordinary. Madonna House does not go to work in any diocese without the invitation of the ordinary of that diocese who, when he invites them, also issues a mandate of the work he desires them to do in that diocese. This mandate is a written agreement between both parties concerning what is required of them and what they will do. It is really a simple bonding in the Lord between the Bishop and the apostolate. Catherine has great love for and respect for bishops. Always she tells her staff: 'When in doubt about anything, go to the Father of your diocese — your bishop — and obtain his direction. He is Christ for you in a special way and through him you will know God's will.'

Upon being asked how they decide upon which places to go to when many bishops are asking for them, the staff say that the Holy Spirit has to decide that. No request is accepted without much prayer and discernment on the part of the community. It is not always the request which may seem most urgent that seems to emerge after prayer as the right one to consider next.

In these field houses the poor are received and taken care of as brothers and sisters of Jesus Christ, for they believe that Christ comes in them. In some houses people are being fed and clothed, the sick are visited, and the staff members join in the evangelisation and pastorale of the local place. The chit-chat apostolate is very important in most of them. This means being available and sharing in many little ways the lives of the people who come. . . it means being a neighbour, a friend, and a helpmate. Some houses are exclusively houses of prayer, adoration, reflection, contemplation. Usually these houses have one or two or more Poustinia rooms where people can come for twenty-four hours and pray and listen to God and fast with just a loaf of bread and some water. . . maybe a cup of tea. Here too, much time is given to listening. People can discuss their problems, pray with a staff member, bring their requests to be prayed for. It is often a sharing of confusions, loneliness, the need for affirmation when one is trying to live the Christian life in a sea of materialism and godless ideals. Some houses are there to be first and foremost a Listening House. Usually the houses are situated in the heart of the masses. Each one is just another house in rows of ordinary houses, in ordinary neighbourhoods, in the stifling greyness of provincial and capital cities.

Some bishops from Canada, the United States, France, Belgium and other countries have requested new foundations. 'God will guide us', Father Callahan told me shortly before his death on 7 April 1984, 'we are in his hands and we will do as he directs by listening to his Spirit by way of his shepherds, the bishops.'

On Christmas Day 1984, I went to greet Catherine Doherty in her cabin which is called St Catherine's. 'Try to be a saintly priest, Father', she whispered, 'and keep loving the Church.' Then I said, 'Give me your blessing.' 'I do not bless you', she said, 'only priests give blessings; but I will place on your head the icon which my holy mother in Russia gave me, and I will ask the Theotokos to take good care of you.'

She took the small icon and pressed it against my forehead while praying aloud to the Madonna of her life, her heart and her apostolate. Then she looked at me with her big, blue eyes and said, 'Give me your blessing, Father'.

Father Omer Tanghe, Pentecost 1985

Postscript

On Sunday, 3 November 1985, I came to Madonna House to visit Catherine in her hermitage. When I entered her log cabin she was sitting at the window, looking out at the waters of the Madawaska River. They were brilliant in the noonday light. She seemed to be looking into eternity. 'Father Omer, one of your associate priests has come to visit you', said Elizabeth, one of the nurses.

I gave her a copy of my book. She looked at it intently and said, 'What's it all about?' 'It's a story about lovers of God — about you and your Madonna House family.' She took my hand, drew me to herself, and gave me a hug. 'Beautiful, beautiful', she whispered.

The following day I celebrated Mass with Father Robert Pelton in St Catherine's hermitage. During the celebration she lay silently on her bed, half dozing, half awake. I knew that, for me, this would be the last time I saw her alive. 'Thank you, Jesus', I prayed, 'for this holy woman, for this mother you have given to us Madonna House priests.'

Catherine died on 14 December 1985, in this same log cabin, and was buried on 18 December. A few weeks later I returned to work, together with Father Bob Wild, on the English translation of this book.

I went to the little graveyard next to the parish church where Catherine is buried. I went to pray at Catherine's grave which was still awaiting her own cross. I prayed, 'I know, Catherine, that you are living now with your Beloved, face to face. Help us to carry on your message of love for the Triune God to the Church, and to all the poor of today's world.'

Father Omer Tanghe, Combermere, 10 January 1986

Appendix

MADONNA HOUSE
PUBLICATIONS

Books by Catherine Doherty

*POUSTINIA
216 pp. soft cover $3.50

Poustinia is the Russian word for desert. Catherine leads us into a deeper dimension of prayer based on the Christian spirituality of the East. She speaks of the Journey Inward during which every soul must arise and take into the heart of her Beloved.

*SOBORNOST
110 pp. soft cover $2.45

A Russian word meaning unity. Catherine continues to draw rich spiritual insight from her heritage, as she speaks of the many meanings of Sobornost. She speaks of the need for the spirit of unity of mind and heart as Jesus spoke of it in the Gospels. 'That all of them may be one, Father, just as you are in me and I am in you.' (*Jn 17:21*)

*STRANNICK
84 pp. soft cover $2.25

Strannick: the call to pilgrimage for Western man, brings to full flower Catherine's reflections on Eastern spirituality for the West. Through this trilogy she reveals that in 'contemplating Sobornost in the Poustinia, one must face being a pilgrim as the outcome.' This is Strannik, the hunger and dream of the pilgrimage that everyone must make to unity with God.

These books are considered a trilogy and were written in this sequence.

MOLCHANIE
100 pp. hard cover only $8.95

The purpose of this book is to describe the only silence that can heal our modern disease — the Silence of God.

URODIVOI
94 pp. hard cover only $9.95

Urodivoi means 'the foolish ones.' In this powerful book Catherine shares her experience of humility as the foundation of the spiritual journey in all times.

THE PEOPLE OF THE TOWEL AND WATER
185 pp. soft cover (with photos) $7.95

The Spirituality of Madonna House. The gospel applied in depth to everyday living.

GOSPEL WITHOUT COMPROMISE
150 pp. soft cover

'If we have the courage to live a life of love with the hearts of children, the world will change.' Catherine goes on to share what that has meant in her own life, what it can mean for all Christians.

FRAGMENTS OF MY LIFE
216 pp. soft cover $3.95

In this book Catherine tells the story of her life, not the purely factual, but rather the story told through her interior vision of how God has led her and moulded her.

DEAR FATHER
84 pp. soft cover $3.95

This book springs from an awesome love for priests and a clear, deep vivid insight into that mystery of faith by which those who really believe that a priest is another Christ.

APOSTOLIC FARMER
24 pp. soft cover $0.75

Catherine remembers the strong lessons she learned from her youth in Russia and explains her vision of the Apostolic Farmer.

I LIVE ON AN ISLAND
126 pp. soft cover $2.75

Catherine lives in a cabin on a small piece of land and from there she shares her visions of the place of the Church in the world today.

DOUBTS, LONELINESS AND REJECTION
93 pp. soft cover $4.50

This is a book which speaks out to our human anguishes and how to find meaning in the Passion, Death and Resurrection of Christ.

NOT WITHOUT PARABLES
187 pp. soft cover $3.95

Stories of faith, some told to Catherine, some she made up herself and some based on incidents that have happened in our Apostolate.

THE GOSPEL OF A POOR WOMAN
187 pp. soft cover $6.95

Catherine shares with her readers the Gospel that has sustained her and led her into the heart of God.

RE-ENTRY INTO FAITH
16 pp. $0.25

Catherine speaks of Faith. The deepest need in our time.

JOURNEY INWARD
116 pp. soft cover $6.95

Journey Inward is taken from Catherine's poetry. It reflects her interior journey over recent decades. Its contents inspire, challenge, and inform. It captures the grandeur and mystery of our union with the Lord of Love.

SOUL OF MY SOUL
128 pp. soft cover $4.95

Catherine shares some of her writings over the years on prayer. It is not a book on how to pray but a book on becoming a prayer.

LUBOV
109 pp. soft cover $5.95

This is the second volume of Catherine's poetry. In it Catherine shares her intimate union with the Beloved. A book to be cherished.

Books by Eddie Doherty

DESERT WINDOWS
$3.95

I COVER GOD
$2.00

HERMIT WITHOUT A PERMIT
$3.50

KING OF SINNERS
$2.00

NUN WITH A GUN
$2.00

SECRET OF MARY
$0.15

118

TRUE DEVOTION TO MARY
$1.50

WISDOM'S FOOL
$3.00

Books by Madonna House members

MADONNA HOUSE AT PRAYER
by Father Richard Starks
$1.00

I MET THE HUMBLED CHRIST IN RUSSIA
by Father Emile Briere
$2.95

HOMILIES IN VERSE
by Father Peter Nearing
$3.95

HE LOVED THE CHURCH
by Father Peter Nearing
$3.95

WORDS FROM POUSTINIA
by Father Robert Wild
$3.95

WORD FROM POUSTINIA Vol. 2
by Father Robert Wild
$3.95

THE POST CHARISMATIC EXPERIENCE
by Fther Robert Wild
$4.50

DESERT HARVEST
by Father Robert Wild
$5.95

Eastern spirituality

THE EYES OF THE GOSPEL
by Archbishop Joseph Raya
$4.50

FACE OF GOD
by Archbishop Joseph Raya
$5.95

JESUS PRAYER, ACATHIST HYMN TO THE NAME OF JESUS
$6.00

Publications in Spanish

POUSTINIA
by Catherine Doherty
$6.00

EVANGELIO SIN COMPONENDAS
by Catherine Doherty
$6.00

Publications in French

DEPUIS LA POUSTINIA (ou le Perlerinage au coeur des hommes)
by Catherine Doherty
$6.95

L'EVANGILE SANS TRANSIGER
by Catherine Doherty
$6.95

POUSTINIA (ou le desert au coeur des villes)
by Catherine Doherty
$5.00

PSAUMES D'UN PECHEUR
by Father Eddie Doherty
$6.95

MA VIE AVEC DIEU
by Catherine Doherty

Subscription publications

RESTORATION
The monthly publication of Madonna House
$2.00 per year

OUR LADY OF COMBERMERE
Medal and pamphlet of story and prayer
Donations: $1.00

These books may be ordered through Madonna House Gift Shop.
Please indicate title, author and price. We would be grateful for a donation to cover postage. Allow 6 to 8 weeks for delivery. Prices correct at time of printing.

Address correspondence to:
> **Madonna House Gift Shop**
> **Combermere, Ontario**
> **KOJ 1LO**
> **Canada**

Many of the books listed above are also available from:
> **Veritas**
> **7-8 Lower Abbey Street**
> **Dublin 1**
> **Ireland**
> **Telephone: (01) 788177**